PORTRAITS OF FAITH

Portraits of Faith

Joel Beeke

BRYNTIRION PRESS

ISBN 1 85049 202 6

Cover design:
Evangelical Press, Darlington

All Scripture quotations are from
the Authorised (King James) version.

Published by Bryntirion Press
Bryntirion, Bridgend CF31 4DX, Wales, UK
Printed by Gomer Press, Llandysul, Ceredigion SA44 4JL

Contents

Foreword

THE annual Evangelical Movement of Wales Conference in Aberystwyth is characterised by the hundreds of young people that crowd the galleries of the Great Hall, many with notebooks and open Bibles, listening intently to the speakers. Some of them are not Christians and, very frequently, this week in which the Bible is taken seriously and explained lucidly to the hearers is a time when the drawing of the Lord Jesus brings them to a knowledge of himself.

So it was in 2003, when Dr Joel Beeke gave these four addresses, examining the state of different people, Adam and Eve, the Shunammite woman, the Canaanite woman, and Caleb, and describing how the Lord who comes searching for us found these very different men and women and brought them to himself.

Almost a year has gone by since I heard these talks, but at regular intervals through these months I have heard of professions of faith in different churches (like one where one of my daughters is a member), which have been attributed to the convicting power of the words that were heard when Dr Joel Beeke spoke in Aberystwyth. Doubts were resolved, questions were answered, clarity was given in areas where hitherto there had been confusion.

Now that the addresses are in print, their usefulness is greatly increased. Ministers like myself will be glad to have such a pastoral tool; Christians young and old will be encouraged and strengthened by reading these delightful pages; and for those with some enquiring spirit concerning the nature of saving faith there could not be a more helpful book to begin.

May God bless this book and increase the impact of its truth to many who were not at Aberystwyth in 2003.

GEOFF THOMAS
June 2004

Introduction

In all our religious speaking, we are sometimes prone to forget the most common concepts and use the most common words without contemplating their meaning. Think of a word like 'grace': we all speak of grace; we declare that we are saved by grace, that our hope is in grace. But do we ever think about what grace means?

That came to me afresh when visiting an aged parishioner in a nursing home. I noticed that in her little room, so greatly curtailed from her former home, she had only one thing hanging on the wall at the side of her bed—a 3 x 5 index card. My curiosity was aroused and I said, 'What do you have on that card?' 'Well, Pastor,' she replied, 'you can go round my bed and see. What I have on that card is my life.' She had the word 'grace' written vertically as an acrostic, and it read:

God's
Riches
At
Christ's
Expense

Let those words sink in—I am sure that is not the full meaning of grace, but it is a good part of its meaning—and have a new refreshing sight of the depths of that glorious word 'grace'.

Faith

Another word we often use without thinking about its meaning is the word 'faith'. We speak of faith; we know that without faith it is impossible to please God; we know that faith is the core and the foundation of daily Christian living. But what *is* faith?

Twenty-nine years ago, I was packing my belongings in Kalamazoo, Michigan, to move to Ontario, where I was to begin studies in our little private denominational seminary as the only student under a local pastor. Now the pastor wanted to know my theological level of knowledge and my writing ability, so when I arrived he said to me, 'Let me give you an assignment right at the start. You can do it in two pages, perhaps five, no more than ten—"What is faith?"'

That's not so difficult, I thought. I had been thinking about faith all of my life and, hopefully, living it for many years. So I went home, rolled up my sleeves and began to work. Come with me now and write the assignment with me for a moment: 'What is faith?'

My first thought was that perhaps I should go to the original language and work off the words used in the Old Testament. As you pastors will know, there are three major Old Testament words for faith, and they mostly mean 'to lean on' or 'to rest in'. Then I could turn to the great New Testament word *pistis*, a word that is used over five hundred times for the faith of the Christian, and describe what it means to trust in the Lord Jesus Christ.

Or perhaps I could base my work on the definition of faith in the Westminster Shorter Catechism. Many of you will know that well: 'Faith in Jesus Christ is a saving grace, whereby we receive and rest upon him alone for salvation, as he is offered to us in the gospel.' What a wonderful framework that would be for a description of faith!

Knowledge, assent, trust

Or maybe I could use the classic Reformed definition of faith, which speaks of its exercise in three distinct acts: saving knowledge, saving assent and saving trust.

Saving *knowledge* would be a wonderful doctrine to develop. I could explain in my paper that you do not just believe with your mind, but with all your heart; you taste faith and you digest it. It is like the old illustration given by Herman Hoeksema of two men sitting down in front of a piece of pizza. One man could not eat it because he had stomach cancer, but he was a nutritionist and knew all the nutrients in it. The other man knew very little; he could see that there was cheese and pepperoni, and he tasted it, ate it and digested it. 'Which man really enjoyed the pizza?' asked Hoeksema. Well, of course, the man who ate it. So I could write about saving knowledge.

Then comes saving *assent*, or agreement. Agreement with who *God* is, in all his wondrous majesty, in his Christocentricity through the Word of God. I could glorify the Father and the Son and the Spirit. I could say with Samuel Rutherford, 'I know not which divine person I love the most, but this I know, I need to know them all and love them all and cherish them all.' And saving assent is agreement, too, with who *I* am: a bankrupt sinner, a poor needy sinner who lives out of Jesus Christ, out of a triune God—a heavenly Father, a redeeming Son, a sanctifying Spirit.

And then, of course, there is saving *trust*, the very heart of faith. That means putting all my confidence in God, putting all my marbles in one basket, trusting in Christ alone and in Christ supremely for salvation. That would make a wonderful way to describe faith.

True and false faith

But, I thought, there must be more. Maybe I should look at faith from the Reformed perspective, and discern true faith from false faith by considering the four types of faith: historical faith— believing with the mind, an outward belief in the Word of God; miraculous faith, believing that something special is going to be done to me or upon me or by me; temporary faith, which seems to rejoice in God for a season but, lacking root, true humility, and genuine Christocentricity, turns back to the world in the day of persecution; and finally, saving faith, which endures and is strengthened under trial.

The inadequacy of definitions

But when I tried all these ways of describing faith, I began to realise that it is something far more rich and comprehensive than all my theological language. It is as embracive as life itself: faith is the heart of our relationship to God; it is the constant central characteristic of the regenerate person. We *live* by faith, says the apostle Paul, and that faith flows from the heart. It is the focal point of my very spiritual existence, the root from which springs all the activity of the believer's entire being.

None of my theological language can get my arms around the depth and the breadth and the height of this glorious thing we call 'faith'. Faith is the activity of the entire heart, the entire life. It is as broad as it is deep; it embraces the weighty matters of personal salvation and the nitty-gritty details of daily living. Without faith, you see, I cannot eat or drink or do all that I do to the glory of God. Without faith, I am always sinning: 'without faith it is impossible to please [God]' (Hebrews 11:6).

Faith is . . .

And then I found John Calvin! Calvin says something like this. Faith is inseparable from Christian liberty. It is inseparable from prayer, from peace, from hope, from love, from repentance, from self-denial. Faith must address the hard questions of life: questions of affliction, of loneliness and despair, of cross providences and numbing trials.

Faith is the heartbeat of evangelism and of missiology. It is the presuppositional basis to my world-view and my life-view. Faith encompasses all that I am. Faith leads me to that grand and glorious vision of the Christian life: 'For of him, and through him, and to him, are all things: to whom be glory for ever' (Romans 11:36). You cannot believe that without faith. You cannot live that without faith. You see, faith is the heart of my relationship to God. It is the heart of life itself. It is the heart of all my theology, especially my soteriology.

You cannot have repentance without faith: they are two sides of one coin. You cannot believe without repenting. In every act of faith we believingly repent and we penitently believe. Without faith, I cannot break with sin—not from the heart. Without faith, I cannot understand the law and its demands and its spirituality, and the joy of walking in the ways of God. I cannot understand the gospel without faith. I cannot understand justification without faith—I receive it only by faith.

I cannot be sanctified without faith. Nothing will work for good in my heart without believing in God. And without faith I cannot go on rejoicing in the indwelling Spirit; I cannot feel the seal of that Spirit in my inward being, for Paul says, 'in whom also after that ye believed, ye were sealed with that Holy Spirit of promise' (Ephesians 1:13). And faith is the principle behind all my truly good works.

Faith works through love (Galatians 5:6), and faith is the necessary condition of all the efficacy of grace. Grace is never efficacious apart from faith; faith is never in competition with grace. *Sola fide* and *sola gratia* walk hand in hand through the pastures of the Word of God, worshipping, adoring and glorifying God. Faith is strengthened by the Word and by the sacraments. The whole field of systematic theology is a field of faith.

Faith in action

I spent forty or fifty hours on this assignment before I wrote one sentence; and yet everything I had done left me unsatisfied. Somehow it was still all too abstract. So I began to search the

Scriptures asking, How does the Bible describe faith? And, of course, I came across Hebrews 11, the great 'heroes of faith' chapter, and saw there how the author handles faith, using it to strengthen the Hebrew Christians when they were discouraged under persecution. I saw how he takes biblical portraits of faith and lays them before his readers, showing from each portrait one or two dimensions of faith, and so, bit by bit, unfolding the richness of its character: 'By faith Abel . . . By faith Enoch . . . By faith Abraham . . .'

And then I began to think, This is the way! You can only understand faith through living biblical portraits, through seeing how faith operates by the Spirit in the lives of fallen sinners like us. And when I understood that, I began to have some breakthrough.

In these four sermons I want to bring you something of that breakthrough. I would like to look at four aspects of faith as they operate in the lives of particular biblical characters—characters who, falling outside the 'hall of fame' (or 'hall of faith') in Hebrews 11, are often forgotten as examples of faith, and yet have so much to teach us. I have chosen them carefully, believing that they demonstrate aspects of faith that the church of Jesus Christ sorely needs today.

As we look at these people, please ask yourselves three questions (and I will ask them of myself as well). First of all, Do I have this kind of faith at all? We need to be honest with ourselves: do we have saving faith? Secondly, Am I exercising the particular aspect of faith that is being expounded? Thirdly, and most importantly, How can this example of this particular dimension of faith be used in my life to mature me in the most holy faith?

Those are the great questions, and I pray God that the Holy Spirit will richly bless these talks, that you may grow as children of God in the grace and knowledge of the Lord Jesus Christ. And if you are not saved, it is my earnest prayer that you will realise the emptiness of life without saving faith and come to see that life without faith in Christ is like a midnight darkness.

A big God—a large life

Without Christ, we are in darkness and are living in a small world. Young people, Satan comes to you, does he not, and says, 'Don't be a Christian! If you become a Christian, your life will be restricted, you'll be in a small world.' But the opposite is true.

When I left the United States army, a sergeant came up to me and said, 'I hope, son, when you go back out into the world, you make it out there in that big world.' I said to him, 'Well, why do you say that to me?' 'Well,' he said, 'because it's a big world. I'm in the army and I serve Uncle Sam; my world is so large because I serve the Government and I've got security. But you, out there in that world all by yourself—you won't have security.' 'Sir,' I said, 'I serve a bigger being than yours. My God is the God of the universe and he will take care of me.'

As a Christian, you do not just serve yourself. If you are not a Christian, you have nothing bigger in your world than yourself, and you are tiny, a speck of dust. Have you ever looked down from a plane and thought that every little human being scurrying about in those little cars below is a speck of dust? But *this* God is the God of the universe, the God who has made billions upon billions of stars and galaxies. And the Christian can say, This God is *my* God! My world is so much bigger, because my God has promised that all things shall work together for good for me, that I may live to his glory through faith.

So faith is the linkage, the pipeline, the instrument by which I am united, in and through Christ, with the great God of the universe. It gives my life breadth and depth and height and meaning. If you are unsaved, your life is small and restricted; but if you are a believer your life is large, because you belong to the heart of a big God.

There was once a little boy, eight years old, who was lying on his deathbed, and his father said to him, 'Son, aren't you afraid to die?' 'No, Dad.' 'Well, wouldn't you want to stay here with us for a while?' 'No, Dad', he said. 'Why not?' 'You see, Dad, when George Whitefield came to town and I heard him preach, and I heard about his big God, ever since then I've wanted to go to be with Whitefield's big God.'

We have a big God not only in this life, but in the life to come. Faith has a big God, and that is what gives the Christian long-term security. The Heidelberg Catechism says it so beautifully: 'What is your only comfort in life and in death?' Life and death— in one breath! You see, of all the comforts that the unconverted believe in and trust in in this world, every single one is only a 'this-life' comfort. The Christian has a 'life-death-eternity' comfort: it is *one* comfort, and it is good for this life, for death, and for eternity—it is good for every situation for ever and ever. As the Catechism says: 'That I with body and soul, both in life and death, am not my own, but belong to my faithful Saviour Jesus Christ; who, with his precious blood, has fully satisfied for all my sins . . .' This faithful Saviour sits at the right hand of the Father to live for me, and to be Lord over my life, so that he may prepare me to be with him where he is.

In these four studies, then, we shall be looking at this big God through the lens of faith, and asking ourselves how this faith is operating in our lives.

1
Adam and Eve: childlike faith

(Genesis 3:20-21; 4:1)

I should like to begin by looking at the faith of Adam and then of Eve, the people who make the first confession of faith in all of Scripture. We shall be looking especially at Genesis 3:20-21, and Genesis 4:1:

> And Adam called his wife's name Eve; because she was the mother of all living. Unto Adam also and to his wife did the LORD God make coats of skins, and clothed them . . . And Adam knew Eve his wife; and she conceived, and bare Cain, and said, I have gotten a man from the LORD.

Adam's faith

'Adam called his wife's name Eve.' These opening words of our text are some of the most remarkable in all of Scripture. I say that because of the tremendous contrast with the previous verse. In verse 19, God says to Adam and Eve, 'In the sweat of thy face shalt thou eat bread, till thou return unto the ground; for out of it wast thou taken: for dust thou art, and unto dust shalt thou return.' The Hebrew word for 'Eve' means 'life', 'life-giver', 'living'. So God says to them, 'You will die', and right on the heels of that pronounced death sentence Adam turns to his wife and says, 'Eve—life'!

Have you ever talked with people who, after you have said something to them, have turned round and said exactly the opposite? And you have said, 'I guess they didn't hear me at all.' Donald Grey Barnhouse wrote that his children would often turn on the radio and flick to different stations. On one such occasion, they had tuned into a station where some royalty was getting married and was being asked, 'Do you hereby take so-and-so to be your wedded wife?' They flicked again and he heard, 'Now go get in your corners and come out and fight!' Barnhouse said that that was like Genesis 3:19 and 20!

The contrast is stupendous. God says, 'You will die', and it is as if Adam does not hear him. He turns to his wife and says, 'Living'; he hears God's death sentence and he pronounces life. And what is still more astonishing is that God does not object and say, 'Adam, didn't you hear me?' He does not reprimand him or correct him.

A life sentence

What is going on here, that Adam's boldness should be un-rebuked? Well, thanks be to God, Adam has also heard Genesis 3:15. For there, in the presence of Adam, God said to the serpent, 'And I will put enmity between thee and the woman, and between thy seed and her seed'—that means your wife, Adam, and all the godly seed that will come from her. Then, suddenly, God turned the plural 'seed' into the singular, and said to the serpent, 'It [the seed—there will be one coming from the woman's seed] shall bruise thy head [Satan, crushing it to death], and thou shalt [do no more than] bruise his heel.'

Now heel-bruising is serious, but it is not fatal. So Adam hears a death sentence (verse 19), but he has also heard a life sentence (verse 15). He has heard of a remedy, a way out, and, facing imminent death because of his sin, he professes simple, childlike faith in the life sentence of God through the seed of the woman.

Seeing that God will bring life through the seed of the woman, Adam turns to her and says, 'Your name shall be Eve, life-giver, for through your loins—how I don't know!—God will bring forth a Messiah.'

Now I wonder if you experientially know in your own heart something of this cry: Eve—life, life in the midst of death! When God the Holy Spirit enters my life and persuades me that I deserve to die, that I am dust, sinful dust, and I must return to dust again, and then throws open the remedy of the gospel for me, and by grace I believe it, repose in it and clasp and grasp it, it is as if I confess with Adam, 'Eve, there is life in Jesus Christ.'

Life in the second Adam

Many years ago in Franklin, New Jersey, I preached a sermon on Genesis 3:20. There was an old janitor in that church who was about seventy years old, and for over twenty years he had struggled to come to liberty in the gospel. That morning he found that his hearing aid was not working. He tried the hearing set of the church but could not get that to work either. So he could not hear a word I was saying. All through the preliminaries and the prayers and the singing he heard nothing. I got to my sermon and announced my text—he heard nothing. But he kept on fiddling around with his hearing aid, and suddenly it came on.

The first words he heard me say were these: 'Eve—there is life in the second Adam, Jesus Christ, for sinners who are on the way to death and hell.' And the Spirit used that one statement to penetrate that man's heart. He broke down and left the church, but he came to see me on Monday and said, 'There is life for me in the Lord Jesus through the promised seed.'

Well, one way or another, perhaps not so dramatically, perhaps more gradually, every believer surely knows the simplicity of this faith, learning simply and sincerely to trust God in his life-giving Messiah.

My dad was nearing his death. He was to have surgery for an aneurysm, and before the surgery he gathered the family around his bed to say farewell in case the Lord took him. He spoke to each one of us, and I will never forget what he said to me: 'Son, please preach the simplicity of the gospel. It is so simple. Adam had one promise, faint though it be, and he believed God, and God counted it to him for righteousness.'

We have thousands of promises. Do we believe God? He gives promises for sinners, for sinners exactly like you and me. The gospel fits each one of us the way a glove fits a hand. It is exactly suited to what you need. 'Eve'—have you ever cried out that there is life in Jesus Christ? There is life in the promises, life abundant.

There was once a prodigal son who went away into a far country, just like the prodigal in the Gospel. He repented, just like that prodigal, and wrote a letter back to his dad. In the letter he said,

> Dad and Mom, I'll be coming on a train through your back yard [the train track went right through their back yard] and as I come around the corner on that train I would love to stop and see you. I know I don't deserve to come home again, but if, as I come around that corner, I see one white sheet out on the line, I'll jump off the train and come home. But if you don't want me home, which I'll understand, don't put any white sheets out.

And when the train came around the corner, the young man could not believe what he saw. Every line had a white sheet; every bush had a white sheet covering it; there were white sheets on the roof, white sheets on the garage, white sheets in the trees, white sheets everywhere. Welcome home, son!

That is the kind of heart God has. It is the heart of the father who ran to meet the prodigal; ran with eyes of mercy seeing him afar off; ran with feet of mercy racing to meet him; ran with lips of mercy kissing him; ran with arms of mercy embracing him; ran with tears of mercy falling upon his boy. He said, 'Bring forth the best robe, and put it on him; and put a ring on his hand [a seal of sonship], and shoes on his feet [a sign of sonship]; and bring hither the fatted calf, and kill it . . . for this my son was dead, and is alive again' (Luke 15: 22-24). He is alive by grace.

Oh, my dear unconverted friend, dear young person, who may be prodigal and away from home, welcome home! Come back, not just to your father and mother, but to the heart of God, to the white sheets of the promises of Scripture. He will welcome you home. He has never yet turned away one sinner who has come to him. 'Him that cometh to me I will in no wise cast out' (John 6:37). If Adam could believe one faint promise (and one that is rather confusing on the first reading), so you ought to be able, by God's grace, to believe in a thousand—ten thousand!—promises in the holy Scriptures.

A wedding song

Eve was the second name that Adam gave his wife. The first name was back in chapter 2: 'Adam said . . . she shall be called Woman, because she was taken out of Man' (verse 23).

Someone has called those words Adam's 'wedding song'. It *is* a kind of wedding song: in Hebrew it is written as poetry, and the Hebrew for 'wo-man' means 'taken out of man'. Adam turned to his wife and said, in effect: 'You are part of me, you are my flesh and blood.' And then verse 24 says, 'they [these two] shall be one flesh.' It is a beautiful wedding song. And Adam joyfully embraces his God-given helpmeet.

But sin interrupts. Sin spoils the first marriage. Sin threatens to wreak utter havoc upon that relationship. Once they have both eaten of the fruit, Adam pretends that he does not even know his wife. He pushes her away. He is no longer intimate with her.

They are no longer best friends. He turns to God with a kind of disparaging comment about her, and even disparages God himself. He says, 'The woman'—he uses his wedding-song name—'whom thou gavest to be with me, she gave me of the tree'—and then, rather meekly—'and I did eat.'

Things are in disrepair. If they continue that way, Adam and Eve are going to be divorced. They are headed for the divorce court. The first marriage is about to break up. But God intervenes in this disaster. He says: Another seed will come, and through this seed, Adam and Eve, you will regain your intimacy, for I will put enmity—*I* will do it—I will put enmity between you and the serpent, and between your seed and the ungodly seed.

So God restores. God undoes what Adam has undone. God interrupts that new league of friendship Adam had made with Satan. He turns it around and re-covenants Adam to himself through his promise.

A song of faith

And so Adam gives his wife a second name, Eve, and the second name is a song of faith, because faith is the evidence of things not seen. Adam does not see the Messiah, but simply, with childlike trust, he believes the promise. He says: I see that in you, Eve, the divine promise will be realised. Life will proceed from your womb. God will carry out his purpose through our seed, and that seed will include a deliverer who will fatally bruise the head of the serpent. And so I see in you, my dear wife, the pledge of divine forgiveness and divine salvation and divine love. Your name is Eve.

Now what amazes me most of all about Adam's simple faith is that he does not offer God any 'ifs' or 'ands' or 'buts' or 'hows'. I say, to my shame, that I am always doing that with God. At times I have sat at my study desk and have actually pounded my fist on the table in anger against myself and said, 'Why don't

I trust thee, Lord? Why these 'ifs' and 'ands' and 'buts'? Why not a simple childlike faith? Hast thou not said that all things work together for good to those that love thee? Why can't I believe it?' Do you struggle like that, too?

Saving faith

'*I will* put enmity . . .', God says. Adam, you do not have to do anything but receive what I say. Faith comes by hearing. Adam has heard; he has believed. He does not even ask for a sign—he is not even a Gideon. He just believes. That is the character of faith. That is what saving faith is all about. Saving faith believes in God. Saving faith surrenders into the evangel, into the arms of God in the gospel, reposing in Christ, clasping Christ, trusting in Christ.

Luther put it this way: 'Faith is the ring that clasps Jesus Christ, who is the diamond.' Faith draws no attention to itself, does it? Our purpose in these four discussions is not to draw attention to faith itself, but to use the characteristics of faith to bring the full spotlight upon our precious Saviour, who gives us, by faith, to live out of him. That is the point of faith.

I am not sure whether you young men in Wales give your fiancées engagement rings when you are prepared to marry them, but in America that is always done. And when the fiancée gets her ring, she shows it off proudly. And it is not 'Look at my ring', but 'Look at my diamond!'

That is what faith does. Adam believes the promise of the Messiah; he gazes upon the diamond of God's promises. When he sees the lustre of the diamond, he loses his 'ifs' and 'hows' and 'buts', just as, when the bride-to-be looks at her diamond, she says, 'Yes, I know my fiancé loves me, because this diamond seals his love.' Jesus Christ is God's seal of love.

And so Adam comes in all simplicity. He does not know the words we know, but he knows there is a word:

Nothing in my hand I bring,
Simply to thy [promise] I cling;
Naked, come to thee for dress;
Helpless, look to thee for grace:
Foul, I to the [promise] fly;
Wash me, Saviour, or I die.

Augustus M. Toplady

Adam's faith puts so many of us to shame. One promise (and a vague one at that) about the coming Deliverer! So little detail! *We* understand it so much better, having the full Bible. And yet Adam says, 'Eve—there is life.'

A hopeless case?

Is anyone thinking, 'But can God look upon me? That was Adam, but what about me? Can God ever look upon me? Such a sinner! You don't know the sins I have hidden in my closet! You don't know how old I am in sin, how hard I am in sin, how severely I've sinned, how I've cast away the gospel invitation countless times, how I've dirtied those white sheets of promise with all my iniquity. Surely God won't have mercy on me?'

You are wrong, my friend. Paul says, 'This is a faithful saying, and worthy of all acceptation, that Christ Jesus came into the world to save sinners' (1 Timothy 1:15). And he adds, 'of whom I am chief'. Can you get beyond the word 'chief'? Yet there is room for you. For everyone there is room. No one is excluded, and if you think that you are so unworthy that God could never have mercy on you, remember Adam. Adam was even more unworthy. In some ways Adam was the greatest sinner who ever lived. He plunged the whole human race into chaos and sin and division and destruction. To this day, all the sin you see in the world around you is the guilt of Adam.

The story is told of the eighteenth-century Scottish preacher Hector MacPhail of Resolis, who for a season encountered

24

great darkness on his deathbed. Many tried to help him, but to no avail. Then one night he had a dream. In the dream he was standing, lonely and dejected, outside the gates of heaven. He heard the sound of people approaching and saw the Old Testament saints walking along, Abraham, Moses and David among them. The gates opened and, amidst shouts of triumph, they walked in. Just as they were walking in, a voice said, 'Hector MacPhail, can you go in with them? Can you go in with David, who committed adultery and murder? Can you go in with Moses, who struck the rock?' Hector MacPhail said, 'Oh, no, Lord, I'm a greater sinner than them all; there's no room for me.' The gates shut, and Hector MacPhail was near despair.

Then along came the New Testament saints, including deny-ing Peter and doubting Thomas. Again the gates were opening, again came the question, and again Hector MacPhail said, 'No, Lord, I'm a greater sinner than them all.'

Then came the ancient church fathers, the Reformers, the Scottish Covenanters. He could not go in with any of them. And along came his own elders and the people in his church. He knew all their faults and weaknesses, their sin and their besetting sins—he had pastored them. And the gates opened and the voice said, 'Can't you come in with them, Hector MacPhail?' 'No, Lord,' he said, 'I'm a greater sinner than them all.'

Finally, there came one lone individual. An old man came hobbling towards the gate, and Hector MacPhail's heart began to pound. 'Are the gates going to open for this man?' he thought. Before the voice came, he said, 'Who is he, Lord? Who is he?' And the voice said, 'This is Manasseh, who filled the streets of Jerusalem from one end to the other with the blood of the saints. Can you go in with him?' And Hector MacPhail awoke from his dream.

Now we do not believe in divine revelation through dreams—we have the full Scripture—but on rare occasions, after we wake, God may apply a dream, using scriptural truths. As Hector MacPhail meditated on that dream, he realised that there was room for the greatest of sinners in the blood of Christ. He called his wife and said, 'Go call the ministers, and tell them that if there's room for Manasseh, there's room for old Hector MacPhail in heaven.'

I say to you that if the last figure in his dream had been Adam, it would have made even more sense, because the blood of all ages rests upon Adam. And if Adam could believe with simple faith in the simple promise of God, do you not have a warrant also for so believing? Why are you not believing? Or rather, what are you believing in? Nothing but the blood of Jesus will do for you. Your sin is too crimson, the dye in the wool is too great; you need the cleansing blood of Jesus Christ.

Eve's faith

Eve also had sinned, and she had sinned first, Paul says (1 Timothy 2:14). She had turned out to be a bad helpmeet, a bad wife. She had interrupted marital harmony; she had destroyed the innocence of the garden; she was involved in the imputed guilt to humankind—not as the covenant head but as one who tempted the covenant head, Adam, to fall. What could Eve expect? At best, she could only expect to become the mother of sinners living under a death sentence—if she were to be a mother at all.

Eve was condemnable. It seemed that there was no future for her but a painful, miserable motherhood: 'in sorrow thou shalt bring forth children' (Genesis 3:16). You women know how painful it is to have a child. God was not lying. It is not enjoyable to go through that pain. What did Eve have but pain for her future, for everything? Who could restore her relationship with Adam? Who could give her obedient children? Who could give her restoration with God?

But suddenly, there in the garden, Adam turns to her and says, 'Eve, there is life.' And Eve receives that promise and believes the song of faith that Adam sings; she believes her own name. How do we know that? Well, we know it from Genesis 4:1: 'And Adam knew Eve his wife; and she conceived, and bare Cain, and said, I have gotten a man from the LORD' (in the original Hebrew, '*the* man from the LORD'). So Eve says, 'Here is the promised seed, the Messiah. This is the one who will deliver us.' Eve is obviously in a frame of faith. Along with Adam, she believes that promise, so that when Adam gives her her name she celebrates with him, and when she receives her first child she believes that the promise of God is on the way—yes, that it has arrived.

So when Adam gives his wife the name Eve, there is little doubt that a new life expectancy surges through the breast of this woman who committed the very first sin. A new hope arises out of the darkness of guilt and sin, a hope that is focused on the promised seed. The tie that now binds Adam and Eve together is stronger than ever before, because it is a tie in the Lord Jesus Christ. Adam and Eve find each other back in the promise.

May I just say a word to young people here? When you look for a helpmeet in life, let it be your first priority to look for a partner with whom you have a common bond in the Lord Jesus Christ, because that tie will last for ever. Beauty—external beauty—will fade: internal beauty will abide for ever. Adam and Eve receive a new cement; their marriage is cemented by the blood of Jesus, the promised seed, and they are bound together inseparably through faith in Christ.

Faith tested

Adam and Eve needed their faith, for they were soon expelled from Paradise, and God's words became true: Adam, you will face thorns and thistles in your hard work, and, Eve, you will experience the pain of child-bearing, and perhaps even more pain in child-rearing. The challenges a mother goes through, rearing children in this sinful world, are unspeakable. How will Eve get through? How will Adam sustain his hard labour? Well, they are cemented through faith in Jesus.

Simple, childlike faith always gets tested, does it not? God delights to test his people in order to strengthen them in the simplicity and childlikeness of their faith. Cain does not prove to be that sinless Messiah. He goes the wrong way. He does things his parents do not want him to do; he says things they do not want him to say. He has a bad temper. What a disappointment! Where is the promise? Is this naughty boy the man from the Lord? What happened to God's promise?

Adam and Eve were so disappointed with Cain that when the second son came along they named him 'Abel', which means 'vanity', 'emptiness', 'transitoriness'. The breath of their expectation was almost knocked out of them. Their faith had not died, we know, but it must have come to a low ebb. Surely they must have struggled when they dealt with Cain as a young boy, as David struggled in Psalms 42 and 43. 'Where is thy God?' the scoffers say. Such a boy, and such a promise!

How can you bring God's providence and God's promise together? You know that struggle in your life; the providences of God seeming to cross lines with the promises of God. Adam and Eve are in a dark tunnel of doubt. And it gets worse before it gets better. Cain rises up and slays his brother Abel. He kills his own brother. Oh, what Adam and Eve go through—the staggering deep waters of cruel murder! Now Cain has gone; they do not know where he is. He is a vagabond wandering somewhere. They have lost him, and they have to bury their other son. Suddenly, they have no children. What now of the promise of this great seed? O God, what of thy promise?

In their better moments, they no doubt say to each other, 'Adam, it's all our own fault. We sinned in the garden.' 'Yes,

Eve, it is our own fault. Let us get down on our knees, my dear wife. Let us cry to God for mercy. Is there yet hope? Is there yet a way to this impossible promise? Is there a way out of this dark tunnel of doubt?'

Faith revived

And Eve becomes pregnant again. What happened? We do not know all that happened, but we do know this: faith has been revived. God's people have their ups and downs and their seasons of doubt. But faith is revived, and when the third son is born Eve calls him Seth—'restitution' (Genesis 4:25). God is restoring what he has taken away. God's promise is not dead. They still believe the simple naked promise of God.

After the birth of Seth, Adam lived for a further 800 years—he was 930 years old when he died (Genesis 5:4-5). Can you imagine how many grandchildren, great-grandchildren, great-great-grandchildren, and additional generations they saw? Imagine how they talked to them all, telling them about the Fall, telling them about the promise, seeing before their very eyes two lines, two seeds developing: the seed of Cain to seven generations, climaxing in that ungodly Lamech, who would kill people out of mere pleasure; and the seven generations of the godly seed, coming to fullness in Enoch, who walked with God and was taken. And they saw in the godly seed that from generation to generation God was fulfilling his promises.

My dear friends, if you have a child or a grandchild who is walking in the ways of God, you have the promise of God in Jesus being fulfilled before your eyes. Praise be to the Lord!

So Eve and Adam begin more and more to see God's promise being fulfilled. They did not know that it would still be some four thousand years before Jesus Christ was born, but they lived out of the promise, not staggering in the midst of adversity.

The gospel made visible

Finally, Genesis 3 shows us one more revelation of the gospel that God gives to help Adam and Eve throughout these long centuries of living by faith. You can find that in verse 21: 'Unto Adam also and to his wife did the LORD God make coats of skins, and clothed them.' God has given the verbal promise in verse 15, and now in verse 21 he gives the visible confirmation, much as we have today in a sacrament.

The shedding of blood

Have you ever stopped to think how Adam and Eve must have felt when God took animals, perhaps lambs, and killed them before their very eyes? Up to that moment there had been no physical death in the whole of Eden.

Recently I was in Brazil, and we were driving down a highway when we saw a dead horse on the side of the road. A horse killed! In America we get used to seeing certain animals, such as deer, dead on the side of the road; we think nothing of it and just try to avoid them. But this occasion was different. There were vultures on top of the horse eating the flesh. What a picture of what we deserve! What a picture of the fruit of sin!

Do you not think that Adam and Eve felt that way when God killed animals before them? They loved God's creation; they were the keepers of that creation. But God killed and shed blood. This was no mere everyday act. This was a solemn moment in the lives of Adam and Eve, and they could not fail to understand the message that 'without shedding of blood [there] is no remission [of sin]' (Hebrews 9:22). And we know they taught that to their children, because Abel came with blood and Cain did not. Cain knew better; he wanted to come before God in a bloodless way.

When God clothed Adam and Eve, he was giving a picture of the gospel. He was telling them: Adam and Eve, your blood will not do, you cannot save yourselves; but I will save you through this seed from the woman, through a way of blood.

Fig-leaf religion

So what does God do? God strips away all their fig leaves. He strips away their fig-leaf righteousness, their filthy, ragged righteousness, and he points them to the white-robed righteousness of his only begotten Son through bloodshed. My dear friends, has that happened in your life? Have you lost all your fig leaves, all your excuses, all your piety, all your repentances? Have you lost everything that you can adorn yourself with before God? Can you say with the writer to the Hebrews that you have become 'naked and opened unto the eyes of him [the living God] with whom we have to do' (Hebrews 4:13) and could not stand before him; that you can only stand before him in Jesus, dressed in his blood and righteousness?

We have to lose our worthiness; we have to lose our unworthiness; we have to lose everything. There are only two religions in the world: there is the religion of fig leaves—the religion of works; and there is the religion of skins—the religion of bloodshedding, the religion of salvation in Christ alone. By nature we all want to meet God with a fig-leaf religion; we all want to stand before him with our churchgoing, our social graces, our kind deeds to our neighbours. We want to come with a clean conscience. But God says: No, come as a sinner. The only true way to come before me is to come just as you are.

Perhaps you have heard that wonderful story of a king who called an artist into his palace and said, 'I'm very bored in this palace. I'm bored with all the decorations. I want you to paint me something that has never been painted and hung in a king's palace before.' The artist went out and found a poor, filthy, bearded, dirty beggar and said, 'Will you come to my studio? I want to paint you.' And the beggar said, 'Yes, I'll come. Just give me a couple of hours and I'll be right there.' The beggar shaved and dressed, and when he was nice and clean he came to the artist. But the artist said, 'I have no need of you now.'

Come as you are

Do not come to God as a Pharisee. Come to him as a publican. Come to him as a sinner. Come to him just as you are, lay your fig leaves before him and say, 'Lord, I'm a sinner. I can't pay for my sins. I can't be perfect. I can't meet any of thy conditions. They can only be met in the Lord Jesus Christ.'

> *Jesus, Thy blood and righteousness*
> *My beauty are, my glorious dress.*
> *Midst flaming worlds, in these arrayed,*
> *With joy shall I lift up my head.*
>
> Nicolaus L. von Zinzendorf
> translated by John Wesley

Believe, friends. 'Believe on the Lord Jesus Christ, and thou shalt be saved' (Acts 16:31). Do not rest, and do not think you are really alive, until you too can cry out as you see the gospel: 'Eve'—there is life in the man from the Lord, the God-man from the Lord, Emmanuel, God with us, the Lord Jesus Christ.

2
The Shunammite woman: submissive faith

(*2 Kings 4:18-37*)

God knows, dear friends, that as Christians we are in desperate need of true submission to all the ways of God. There was a woman in America, a Christian woman, who was very rebellious at some of the ways of God, and on one occasion she said to God, 'I would trade my cross for anyone else's.'

That night, the woman had a dream, in which everyone in her block put their crosses out on their front lawns. She went to the first cross, but when she saw it she said, 'I think I'll pass on this one, I'll try another.' On she went from cross to cross, but passed on them all. Finally coming to a home where there was no cross on the front lawn, she went to the door and rang the bell. When a woman came to the door, she said, 'May I trade my set of afflictions with yours? You can take my crosses and I'll take yours.' The woman replied, 'Honey, you don't want mine; mine are too big to get out the door.'

When this woman awoke, she realised that her rebellion was out of place. She saw that God's cross was just right for her; she had no business trying to change God's providential leadings with her, but needed submissive faith to trust in his ways.

Dear friend, if you are a Christian, I say to you without any hesitation that God has never made one mistake with you in your entire life. He has never given you one cross too many or one cross too few. He has never given you a cross that did not profit you. What you need is daily, genuine, submissive faith: faith to say amen to God's ways, faith to receive what he in his inscrutable wisdom deems fitting to put upon you. You need faith to trust him with every affliction.

Look back just a moment and scan your life. Has the Lord ever done you ill? Why are some of us chafing under our present crosses? The world today abhors submission; the very word is degraded. But it is a beautiful word in God's eyes, and what need there is for it! Martin Luther said: 'Letting God be God is half of all true religion.' Bowing under God's ways lies at the heart of true and vital Christianity; it is the heartbeat of that rare jewel (as Jeremiah Burroughs put it) of Christian contentment.

An inventory
So now I want us to take an inventory. An inventory does three things: it helps a business look at its present stock, its present condition; it helps a business look at its past to see how well it has done; and it helps a business look at the future to see if continuing in its present direction will be profitable. I want you, then, to come with me, and I pray the Holy Spirit that he will enable every one of us (myself included) to take a spiritual inventory of where we are, where we have come from, and where we are going, with regard to this cardinal issue of daily submissive faith.

With God's help, I want to look with you at two verses in 2 Kings 4:

> And she said, It shall be well . . . Run now, I pray thee, to meet her, and say unto her, Is it well with thee? Is it well with thy husband? Is it well with the child? And she answered, It is well (verses 23, 26).

We have seen that one of the best ways to grasp various aspects of saving faith is to study biblical portraits of faith. And we have committed ourselves to looking at portraits that are not commonly considered, portraits that are not specifically included in Hebrews 11 (although they are there implicitly, of course, because the author of the letter to the Hebrews says that there are many others who live by faith). From those 'many others' we are picking out five people whose lives particularly address four aspects of faith sorely needed today, aspects in which we are severely short-changing ourselves when we ignore or reject them.

We have seen that although Adam, as our covenant head, was responsible for plunging the entire human race into sin (Romans 5 and 1 Corinthians 15) and thus, as covenant head, stands in opposition to Jesus Christ, yet God overruled the seriousness of the great sin committed by both Adam and Eve, granting them stupendous, amazing grace to believe the promises of God.

We saw too that Adam and Eve are examples of simple, child-like faith, a faith sorely needed in the world today. They had only one promise, but they responded to that one, while we often let the thousands of promises we have go by. One old Puritan, William Spurstowe, in his wonderful book on the promises of God, *The Wells of Salvation Opened*, wrote that the promises in Scripture are like a big bag of golden coins, and when you open the Bible God takes that bag, unties the strings and throws the coins at your feet, saying, 'Take what you will.' Well, Adam and Eve took the one golden coin God gave them.

When trouble comes

In our first inventory, we asked whether we have Adam and Eve's simple and childlike trust in God. But now we need to ask the question: How do we live out that faith day by day, particularly in times of trouble, affliction, sorrow and need?

Saved or unsaved, we all face those times: 'man is born unto trouble, as the sparks fly upward' (Job 5:7). That is part of our inheritance as children of the first Adam. So I do not ask you, 'Are you afflicted?' or 'Have you been afflicted?' We know the answer. Everyone has their crosses. You have your own set. You have been afflicted, and at certain times in your life those afflictions have been more intense than at other times, have they not? Nor do I ask you where these afflictions have come from. That is not the real question. You know where they come from. You know they are traceable back to our fall in Adam, back to sin, ultimately. You know too, if you are a Christian, that they are sent to you by a wise and a fatherly God.

The real question is this: How are you responding to afflictions? Are you running from them? Are you cowering before them? Are you trying to get out of God's gymnasium, in which he is training you under his afflicting rod? Or are you submitting by faith to all God's dealings with you? Do those around you— your spouse, your parents, your children, your friends—see the vitality of God's presence, of your Christianity, by the way you respond to afflictions?

The world watches Christians very closely, and never so closely as when God in his inscrutable wisdom deems it fitting to put them in the furnace of his affliction. And if you are a Christian who is really walking with God, you know what it means to struggle with this critical question: Lord, how can I live as a Christian under affliction? How can I honour thee in affliction? How can I respond to it rightly by being prepared for it before it comes, by walking in a godly way when it is resting upon me and, after it is over, by looking back gratefully upon it?

If you are like me, you do not worry too much about God taking care of you in the afflictions that will come, but you *are* concerned about how you can honour God in your afflictions. You are concerned about how to avoid being like the world. You want to have a better conviction, a better philosophy, a better approach to affliction than simply saying that you resist it, or stoically saying that you have to grin and bear it. When God's afflictions come, how can I respond as a Christian? How can I live *soli Deo gloria*—giving glory only to God—so that God alone is magnified in my life? That is the question.

Of course, to honour God in our lives, we need the Holy Spirit: you know that, and I know that. But the Spirit is as willing to give himself as Christ was willing to give himself on the cross, and as willing as the Father was to give the Son. So the real question is: How does the Holy Spirit work this? How does he make me willing, and how can I respond to these overtures and these leadings so that, in affliction, my life reflects the glory of God through the Spirit by faith?

The Shunammite woman is a mentor for us. As we look at her life, we will consider, first, her submissive faith for the future; secondly, her submissive faith in the present; and thirdly, some applications for us.

'It shall be well'

We go in our thoughts to a little city named Shunem, five miles north of Jezreel. (Called Solam today, Shunem still exists; it is a small village fifteen miles from Mount Carmel.) Elisha was in the habit of stopping here from time to time on his way to Carmel, where he gave theological lessons to a school of the prophets who resided there. When he went through the village of Shunem he customarily stayed at the home of a great woman, a woman great in faith.

The gift of contentment

Already in the opening verses of the story of the Shunammite woman we discover things about her that we admire greatly. Elisha is so grateful for her hospitality that he asks his servant Gehazi to try to find out something she might desire, so that he can give her a return favour. But the woman responds, 'I dwell among mine own people' (2 Kings 4:13).

That is an amazing response. The woman is childless, and you know what it was not to have children in Bible times: it was thought to be a sign of God's finger of judgement against you. Every woman wanted a child, and cherished the secret hope that in her loins might be the Messiah. Childlessness was often considered to be one of God's greatest curses. And yet, when Gehazi asks her, this woman makes no mention of her childless condition. She simply says that she dwells among her own people. She has the rare jewel of godly contentment—and what a blessing that is! What a blessing it is to see a child of God living under crosses and fully content with the ways of God!

May I ask you, as part of the inventory, do you 'amen' the ways of God in your life, even when they are against your flesh? Can you say, 'I'm just content to dwell among the people of God'?

The child of promise

You know, of course, that Elisha does something amazing: he prophesies that in one year's time the Shunammite woman will have a son. And, much to her astonishment after all those years of childlessness, it happens, and the lad grows up and is the joy of the mother and, no doubt, of the father too. He is a child of promise, a child sent by God, a special child.

When he is perhaps ten or twelve years old, the mother sends the child out to work with his dad in the field. One day the boy feels ill—he probably has sunstroke. His head begins to hurt very badly and he says to his dad, 'My head, my head' (verse 19). Not realising the seriousness of the headache, the boy's dad says to one of his workers, 'Carry my son home to his mother.' The child comes to the mother, sits on her knees until noon . . . and dies! Her only son, the son of promise, the son whom God has so wonderfully given, the son who symbolises everything to this woman about God's covenant faithfulness—that he is a God of impossibilities and a God of goodness and of kindness—this only son dies! He was given so miraculously, and now, taken so early. You can imagine the questions: Was this all in God's disfavour? Did God give us this child to torment us? What is God saying?

To lose a child is one of the greatest struggles in life. I have seen people cry hard when they have lost a parent, but the hardest tears I have ever seen as a pastor have consistently been when parents have had to go the unnatural way of bringing their own children to the grave. Oh, what a trial! Lord, must it be so? Lord, how can this all work together for good? My only son, dead!

The response of faith

What does this woman do? We are told, 'She went up, and laid him on the bed of the man of God, and shut the door upon him, and went out' (verse 21). She does three things, and all three are acts of faith.

First, she puts him on the bed of the man of God. That is astonishing, because in Israel anything that came into contact with the dead was considered unclean. So here we have the first hint that this woman believes that somehow the God of Elisha is going to raise her son from the dead. Otherwise why would she go to that special chamber, which she has particularly added on to her home for the prophet, and make it unclean? Certainly there is nothing anywhere in this chapter to indicate that she is acting out of rebellion or enmity against the prophet. She lays her son on the bed of the man of God because she believes that the God of Elisha, the God who wondrously gave her this son, is able wondrously to raise him from the dead. So here already we see her faith.

Secondly, the mother shuts the door on her son. That, too, is remarkable. In Bible times, with the hot climate, when someone died, preparations had to be made immediately for the burial, which often took place the same day. There was a lot to do: mourners had to be hired; people had to be gathered; word had to be sent. This woman shuts it all off. You would almost want to tap her on the shoulder and say, 'Shunammite woman, I know you're distressed, but do you realise what you're doing? Suppose someone finds your son dead while you've gone to see the prophet fifteen miles away at Mount Carmel? People will say, "What kind of a mother are you, to abandon a dead child?"'

She shuts the door upon him. She does not want anyone to find him; she does not want the mockers to have their gainsaying hour; she does not want the enemies of God and the false prophets to rejoice in the death of her son. She believes and she submits at the same time.

And then, thirdly, she goes out. She goes out by faith. She is tried to the point of extremity, and yet she is driven out of herself to Elisha—and this, of course, symbolically, means to the God of Elisha—for help and for solution.

But then there is another trial. Elisha is fifteen miles away, and in Bible times women were not supposed to take long journeys by themselves. But never mind. Faith is enormously inventive; it climbs over walls; it climbs on roofs. (Remember the four men who climbed on the roof and let the paralysed man down at the feet of Jesus?) Nothing stops faith: it drives on; it must have communion with God; it must be in his presence. She sends a message to her husband: 'Send me, I pray thee, one of the young men, and one of the asses, that I may run to the man of God, and come again' (verse 22). Her husband responds, 'Wherefore wilt thou go to him to day? It is neither new moon, nor sabbath.' Another obstacle! But she says, 'It shall be well.'

'*Shalom*'

The woman does not write a lengthy explanation; she does not have a long dialogue with her husband and justify herself by

40

giving him all the details of why she is going. She says (in Hebrew) one word, '*Shalom*' (Peace). Peace, with your only son dead at home? Is she being hypocritical? Is she trying to hide something from her husband? '*Shalom*'—'It shall be well.' The word is future orientated: God will make it well; I will trust him for the future. The God who has been faithful in the past will be faithful in the future, and no matter what he does or what he does not do, I trust him. That is the language of submissive faith. I believe in God more than I believe in myself. That is the mark of great faith.

When we become Christians we can easily say we believe in God and trust him, but often, in practice, we trust ourselves more than we trust God. But this woman says, '*Shalom*'—'It shall be well.' The God of Elisha will take care of me as I travel fifteen miles to and fro, and he will take care of my son. He will take care of everything, dear husband. Don't worry. Our God lives; the God of Elisha lives. So the Shunammite woman sets off: 'She saddled an ass, and said to her servant, Drive, and go forward [she uses the means]; slack not thy riding for me, except I bid thee.' So she comes to the man of God at Carmel.

Do you use the means and, as you use them, trust God to make everything well in your future? Think about what you worry about most right now, something that has not happened but may happen. Can you say, 'It shall be well, because my expectation is in the Prince of Peace, in the Lord Jesus Christ. He is our *Shalom* and my trust is in him—not just in a thing, but in a person, an almighty person'? That *shalom* is certain. 'It *shall be* well'; not may be, not 90 per cent sure. God is faithful. It *shall be* well.

'It is well'

Elisha sees the woman a long way off and sends Gehazi. He tells him to run to meet her and say, 'Is it well with thee? is it well with thy husband? is it well with the child?' (verse 26).

And she answers, 'It is well.' It *is*! Now it took great faith for the Shunammite woman to believe that God would raise her son from the dead, and that all *would be* well. But I submit to you that it took greater faith to say, 'It *is* well.' This is the heart of submission in the midst of faith.

True submission

I want to grapple for a few moments with this whole question of submission. What really is submission? When we look back on our past, we ask the question, What does it mean to submit to God's ways? I want to suggest to you that true submission involves four things—four steps, if you will—which I believe go deeper as we go along. Then, having shown by these four steps what submission is, I will show you what it is not, because there are misconceptions about that as well.

Acknowledging that it is the Lord

The first step in true submission is that I acknowledge that all my afflictions are from the Lord.

After 9/11, John MacArthur was in an interview on a television station along with three other ministers and a rabbi. When Larry King asked the question, 'Was God's hand in this?' the other four basically said, 'No. God could not have anything to do with this.'

But I say to you that if God has nothing to do with your affliction, then you cannot go to him for refuge as you deal with it. You have no answer. You have nothing more than stoic hardness. The very best you can do, therefore, is grin and bear it, hoping that somehow you may get back under the control of a God who seems to have no control over you and what happens to you. If God's hand is not in your afflictions, directing them, you have an impotent God. You have a God who cannot save you, a God who cannot deliver you. There is no comfort in that at all.

42

So when affliction comes in your life, the very first thing you should say is this: 'It is the Lord. Lord, what art thou saying to me?' Submission bows toward the Lord. It is not like that crowd who came with their lanterns and torches and weapons to capture Jesus in Gethsemane. When he came forward and said, 'I am he', they fell backward away from him. But when we submit, the direction of our life is *toward* the Lord. We turn to him, we want his will, we want his guidance. We say right away, 'It is the Lord.' Obviously this Shunammite woman realised that, otherwise she would not have gone straight to the prophet. She knew it was the Lord; the same God who gave was the God who had taken away.

Agreeing that the Lord is right
The second step in true submission is to justify the Lord in all that he does. It is one thing to say, 'It is the Lord': it is another to say, 'It is right. I deserve it. I deserve worse.' To justify God in all his doings is an important part of true submission, of true faith.

What did Aaron say when God took away his sons? Nothing: he 'held his peace' (Leviticus 10:3). But in that holding of his peace there was language, was there not? It was not just a stoic hardness, it was the language of submission. It was righteous.

When Samuel told Eli that his sons would be taken from him, Eli said, 'It is the LORD: let him do what seemeth him good' (1 Samuel 3:18).

When David was taken from his throne by his own son, he said, 'Behold, here am I, let him do to me as seemeth good unto him' (2 Samuel 15:26).

And when Job lost all ten of his children at once—imagine that!—he did not say, 'Lord, couldn't I have kept one?' He said, 'The LORD gave, and the LORD hath taken away' (Job 1:21). Submission testifies that God is right!

At one time in my ministry I was being falsely accused of some horrible things. There was not a speck of truth in these accusations, yet they were being spread throughout the churches. It was dreadful, and I was bitter, and I did not take it to the Lord as I should. But, finally, it broke me and I went into my study and just cried to the Lord: 'Lord, have mercy.'

Then I began to see who I was, and how much wrong I had done in my life, and how I deserved much greater condemnation. I went over to a shelf and picked out a book. After I had read a page or two, I came across a passage in which the author said, 'Perhaps some of you are going through very difficult times because you have been falsely accused and people are saying lies about you.' I was just astonished. He continued, 'Then thank the Lord, because if the people spreading those rumours knew who you really are, they would have far worse things to talk about. You deserve a lot worse.' You see, we are a lot worse than we ever get treated. God is always better to you and to me than we are to him. He is always better than we deserve.

When I was twelve years old, something rather miserable happened in our family, and I was complaining and groaning to my mother, as a twelve-year-old can. But she just kept saying, 'Well, it could be worse; it could be worse.' She had been saying that for years! Everything that happened 'could be worse'. Finally I got upset with her and I said, 'You know, you can say that about everything—"could be worse".' She said, 'That's right, son, because we deserve hell, and anything above death and hell is the mercy of God. It could always be worse. When I see who I am and what I deserve, I have no reason to complain, *ever*.'

I have a theological student, a single man in his upper twenties, who has been praying for a God-fearing wife for several years now. He has read the best marriage books on the market, and feels God has prepared him for marriage. Some months ago he felt that the Lord was leading him to court a particular young lady. He came to me to ask my opinion; he went to the father, and it was fine with him. Everything is in order. He comes and talks to me two or three more times. His heart is set on this girl. I pray with him, he prays with me, and he speaks to the girl—and she agrees to court him. He is deeply grateful. She is a wonderful girl, a God-fearing girl; there is a wonderful spirit about her; she is a gem. He is so happy.

It lasts three weeks! One day someone comes to me and asks if I have heard. I say, 'No, what?' 'It's all off.' 'Oh,' I say, 'he must be heartbroken.' 'You'd better talk to him.' So next time he comes in I say, 'Come into my study a moment, my friend. It's tough, isn't it?' 'Oh,' he says, 'the Lord showed me that a child of the King ought never to complain. I'm well, Pastor, because I didn't deserve her anyway.'

Submission! It is right. No matter what he does to me, it is always better than I deserve.

Approving that it is well

But submission goes deeper. There is a third step. True submission approves of the Lord. You see, it is one thing to say, 'It is the Lord'; another to say, 'It is right'; and another again to say, 'It is well.' Job did not just say it was right; he did not just say, 'The LORD gave, and the LORD hath taken away'; he also said, 'Blessed be the name of the LORD' (Job 1:21). That is the astonishing thing. To see who I am and accept that I am a lost sinner before God, that is a miracle. But to approve, to 'amen' the ways of God with me when they are against me, or seem to be against me, goes far, far deeper. 'Blessed be the name of the LORD.'

'How is it with your child?' 'It is well!' I submit. I approve of God's ways. What an amazing thing this is! Sometimes, as a pastor, you are amazed at the people who do not have this spirit, though they have been long on the way; and you are amazed, sometimes, at the people of God who do have this spirit, even when they have only been a little while on the way.

Not long ago I had a woman in my church who had just received word that she had a rather dangerous kind of cancer. I went to see her, of course, right away. When you serve a fairly large church, there are times when your work as a pastor can overwhelm you. At that particular time we had several people in the church with cancer, and during that period there were times when a dozen or more people were in hospital. So I stood out in the hallway, knowing before I went into the room that I was about to enter a situation in which I would have to invest many an hour, many a prayer. I cannot explain it to you, but pastors know. When you go through this with a person over months and years, you go on a roller-coaster ride. There is emotion; there are tears and prayers; there is a real closeness to the person that is wonderful. But so much energy has to go out from a pastor in such cases.

On that occasion, as I stood out in the hall, I felt overwhelmed. I said, 'Lord, help me to become fully engaged in my mind and soul, to deny myself as I enter this room and throw myself into this situation with a pastoral heart.' I'll never forget what I heard as I entered the room: 'How are you, Pastor?' 'How am *I*? How are *you*, my friend? Having a rough time?' 'Oh no, Pastor, this is really special.' 'Special! Cancer—special?' 'Yes, special.' 'Why special?'

Well, you see, Pastor, God is dealing with me, and that's good news, isn't it, because I've got such a wayward heart. And besides, now that I have cancer, my family will be coming to see me, and my friends as well, and I'll have an opportunity to tell them and show them how wonderful God is. And didn't you tell us, Pastor, that God makes no mistakes, and all things work together for good? So this cancer he's

46

going to use, isn't he? And, Pastor, one more thing: I want to
be his disciple.

(This was a babe in grace talking—she had only been converted
two years before that.)

I want to be his disciple, and to be his disciple I have to be disciplined, don't I? And to be disciplined with my hard heart I
need affliction. So this is God's gift to me. Pastor, it is well
with my soul.

Now don't you go around worrying about me. God is going
to take care of me. I am well.

When I left the room that first time, I thought, 'Well, that's a
wonderful beginning, but I know enough about pastoring to know
that in a few months' time there might be a different language,
when the pain is intense and morphine is needed, and the chemo
is repetitive.' But that woman went through her whole bout of
cancer speaking this way the whole time. I never met her not
thanking God for her cancer.

If every person who is a true Christian would respond in this
way to affliction, what a difference it would make! Would God
use it to bring revival? Would God use it to bless and saturate
the churches with the reality of Christianity? Oh, how we need
submissive faith!

Cleaving to him as my Friend
But there is yet one more step. The fourth step of submission is
cleaving to the Lord, cleaving to him as my greatest friend when
he seems to come out against me as my greatest enemy. Have
you ever seen a man with a very faithful dog? The man can tease
the dog and throw a stone or stick at him, but the dog will run and
bring it back. If you are truly submissive, you will take God's
sticks and stones and you will bring them back to him. You will

47

cling to him, and cleave to him, and treat him as your greatest friend, no matter what he does to you.

Job reached that position, at least at certain points in his suffering. Sometimes he wandered away and his faith grew weak. But there was a time when he said, 'Though he slay me, yet will I trust in him' (Job 13:15).

One of the dearest saints in my church is dying; I am expecting a phone call any day. This woman has been in hospital scores of times in the last fifteen years, and she, too, is a remarkable example of submissive faith. God applied to her soul the words, 'My times are in thy hand' (Psalm 31:15), and she has asked me to speak on those words at her funeral. In the last few weeks she has reached the point where her mind is not good any more. The last time I saw her, just before I got on the plane to come to Wales, she said to me:

Pastor, I know that my mind is going in and out. I know that some things I say are not making sense to you, but don't worry about that. Just take what makes sense and let the rest go. I want you to know before you go on your trip that the one thing that has never left me is that he is mine and I am his, and though he slay me it will only be to take me to himself. It is all well.

In the last few years, that woman has pastored me a lot more than I have pastored her. How sweet it is to see an afflicted friend cleaving to God! At times I have walked to her hospital room and, coming around the corner and standing at the door, I have heard her voice and seen her face contorted with pain, and I have not known whether to walk in or go away. But she would spot me and say, 'Oh, Pastor, it's all right; it's nothing compared to what my Master suffered for me', and she would replace the distorted look with a smile.

You and I are often not like that, are we? We are frequently like Jonah. Some little gourd is taken away from us and we say, 'I do well to be angry, even unto death' (Jonah 4:9). And we excuse ourselves in some way: 'I can't help it. I've got a temper. This is the way my father was.'

All those excuses! That is the world talking; that is your old nature talking. It ought to bother us that we are not submissive. It ought to drive us to the Lord. We ought not to rest until we can say, 'I bow *toward* the Lord because it is the Lord. I bow *before* the Lord because I justify him. I bow *under* the Lord because I approve of him. And I bow *in with* the Lord and cling to him.' That is true submission.

But how can you get that submission? Well, the Shunammite woman did not have it in her own strength either. We are all rebels, especially when we do not realise who we truly are. How did she realise that? How could she live this way? How could she say, 'It is well'? How could she cling to the God of the prophet?

The supreme example

The submission of the Shunammite woman was, of course, because of Jesus Christ. How much of that she understood we do not know, but we do know from our New Testament perspective that it is only because of Jesus that we can experience these four steps in submission. It is only because Jesus went through them, only because he was the submissive one *par excellence*, only because he said of whatever happened to him, '*It is the Lord.*'

When he was twelve, Jesus said, 'Wist ye not that I must be about my Father's business?' (Luke 2:49). He was always conscious of his Father, conscious in every step he took that he had to be doing the work of the one who had sent him: 'My Father worketh hitherto, and I work' (John 5:17).

And Jesus always *justified God*, did he not? He saw all his sufferings as coming from the hand of a just God. He was suffering for the unjust. That is why as a Lamb he could not speak. He did not answer Pilate because he, the innocent one, was taking the place of the guilty, so that the guilty might be set free.

> He was oppressed, and he was afflicted, yet he opened not his mouth: he is brought as a lamb to the slaughter, and as a sheep before her shearers is dumb, so he openeth not his mouth . . . [Why? Because] he was wounded for our transgressions, he was bruised for our iniquities: the chastisement of our peace was upon him; and with his stripes we are healed.
>
> (Isaiah 53:7, 5)

Then Jesus Christ *approved of the Lord* even in his greatest sorrow: crawling as a worm in Gethsemane; forgotten by his own disciples who could not watch with him one hour; no eye to look upon him; no one to give him a glance and say, 'Lord we understand'; bleeding sweat. 'Father, if thou be willing, remove this cup from me' (Luke 22:42). Bearing all the hell that his elect deserve for all eternity, all their sins being pressed down upon him, he said, 'nevertheless not my will, but thine, be done'. It is well!

And he *cleaved to the Lord*. The one who was the apex of all human history, and the culmination of all human suffering, was forsaken of God, forsaken of man, forsaken of nature—even the sun would not shine upon him. In the midst of the darkness and agony and soul dereliction, he cried out, 'My God, my God, why hast thou forsaken me?' (Matthew 27:46). He was still clinging to God, though God pushed him away with both hands. He reached out with open hands on the cross and said, 'My God, my God'. It is because of Christ we can be submissive, and it is to Christ we must go for submission.

'Learn of me,' he said, 'for I am meek and lowly' (Matthew 11:29). Is it well with you? Are you submissive? Have you learned submission? Have you submitted your whole life to God? Is there any besetting sin, bosom sin, darling sin, clinging to your life that you have not surrendered and submitted to God, and have not forsaken and fled from? There is nothing that will damage our lives so much as clinging to bosom sin; it will kill submission.

What submission is not

There are lessons here, too, about what submission is not. Let me give you three of them.

Not stoicism

Notice that when the Shunammite woman comes to the man of God and catches him by the feet, Gehazi comes near to thrust her away. But the man of God says, 'Let her alone; for her soul is vexed within her' (2 Kings 4:27). She is 'vexed'—does that sound like submission? Yes! Christian submission is not stoicism. It is *not* not feeling the affliction.

A woman once came to me who had lost her husband a few years earlier, and she said, 'I'm doing just fine. God gave me such submission that my husband's death never bothered me and I never missed him.' I did not know what to say! Sometimes Christians respond that way. They say that God has taken away the burden (that is the way they look at it), and because of that they do not have any struggle whatsoever. And they think that that is submission. Now I grant that at certain times God may take away a burden in a special way, but if something causes you no trouble, you do not need to submit to it, because it has not bothered you to begin with. True submission is to 'amen' God's way when the affliction lies heavy upon you; it is truly denying yourself and taking up the cross and following him.

Not closing your mind to questions

True submission is not avoiding seeking the reason for God's providential dispensation. Now many people have said to me (and I have thought a lot about this, and actually believed it myself when I was young) that we cannot ask God why. I am often asked, 'Is that right?'

Well, yes and no. You cannot shake your fist at God and shout, 'Lord, why art thou doing this?' But you can ask this way: 'Lord, search me and know my heart, and try me, and root out every evil way within me, and lead me in the way everlasting.' If you think it is true that you can never ask God why something has happened, then what do you say about Jesus, who asked the greatest 'why' question ever asked: 'Why hast thou forsaken me?' (Matthew 27:46)?

When you feel forsaken of God and you go to him in earnest, desiring him, panting after him as a hart pants after the waterbrooks, you may say, 'My God, why hast thou forsaken me?' That is what this Shunammite woman does. She falls at Elisha's feet and says, 'Did I desire a son of my lord? did I not say, Do not deceive me?' (verse 28). I don't understand. Why is this happening?

Not fatalism

And then, finally, true submission is not sitting back with folded arms saying, 'The Lord's will be done, whatever be done. If the Lord comes, he comes; if he doesn't, he doesn't; and so I'll go my own way.' No! This woman is not happy with Gehazi being sent. She says to Elisha, 'As the LORD liveth, and as thy soul liveth, I will not leave thee' (verse 30).

Now the woman does not know Gehazi well. We, however, do know a little bit about him, and I am not sure I would trust him either! She sees Elisha as the representative of God and, in her mind, staying with Elisha represents clinging to God. She is willing to let Gehazi go on ahead, but Gehazi with Elisha's staff is not enough for her. She stays with Elisha: 'As the LORD liveth, and as thy soul liveth, I will not leave thee.' Submissive faith wrestles with God even as it bows before him: 'I will not let thee go, except thou bless me' (Genesis 32:26).

And so Elisha and the woman go together. You know the rest of the story, of course. Elisha lays himself upon the boy; the boy sneezes and opens his eyes; Elisha delivers him to his mother. And then we read verse 37, that wonderful closing verse: 'Then she went in, and fell at his feet, and bowed herself to the ground, and took up her son, *and went out*'—it is the second time we read those words, but this time she is holding her child. The God of whom she proclaimed, 'It shall be well', the God of whom she proclaimed, 'It is well', is the God of whom she can now say, 'He hath done all things well' (Mark 7:37).

For us today

In conclusion, then, what does this story have to do with us here and now? Well, my dear friends, there is one place to go for submission, and that is, as I have already said, to the Lord Jesus Christ. I want to conclude by telling you, first, why it is such a grievous offence in God's sight not to go to him, and secondly, and very briefly, how to go to Jesus Christ for submission.

Refusing to submit

To refuse to go to Jesus for submission flies in the face of Jesus Christ's submission. Shall an innocent, holy, perfect Saviour, who suffered for me, submit to his Father's will even to the death of the cross, and I not be willing to suffer even a little bit for his sake? Do you see what an offence that is?

A few weeks ago, a father took his son golfing. Ten minutes after they returned home, his wife came to him and said, 'You just took our son golfing, and now he's grumbling because he has to do some chores.' The father took him into a side room and said, 'Son, I just spent a whole morning golfing with you. You thanked me for it, didn't you?' 'Yes', he said. 'Well, why are you grumbling about doing chores now?' 'Oh,' he said, 'I'm sorry, Dad.'

But that is what we are like as Christians, and it is terrible. Jesus Christ does everything for us; he suffers, dies and agonises for us—for us who deserve the curse and wrath of God. And then we grumble when we have a few chores to do, and a few sufferings to bear. Who do we think we are?

Secondly, not to submit is so grievous to God because it means that we are really saying, 'My Father in heaven doesn't know what's best, he doesn't know how to rule my life.' My lack of submission is nothing but rampant, sinful, godless humanism. It is saying that I want to be captain of my own ship, and master of my own fate. It is not believing our Lord when he says, 'What I do thou knowest not now; but thou shalt know hereafter' (John 13:7). 'Do not be anxious about anything,' says Paul. True Christians ought not to be in the worrying business, because their Father knows best.

Thirdly, a lack of true submission is symptomatic of a lack of self-knowledge, even as it gives a poor testimony to the world. Those who do not submit show that they do not know themselves.

You see, young people, contrary to what the world says to you, the only truly happy people in this world are the people who realise the curse of God and the wrath of God against sin, who see their own sinfulness over against that wrath and know that they do indeed deserve nothing but death and hell. They are the only truly thankful people, because they know that whatever they receive is above what they deserve. If you think that you have good things coming, and that you have earned them and deserve them, then you are not happy when they come. 'Well,' you say, 'I earned it.' But if you are amazed by what you receive because it does not compare with what you deserve, then you are content.

I told you about my mother, who said that anything above hell is a gift. My mother is one of the happiest people I know on the face of this earth, because she lives that out. When we do not submit, we reveal that we are thinking far too much of ourselves and far too little of God's disciplinary paternal hand upon us. As Hebrews 12 puts it, God disciplines us in order to wean us from this world and ripen us to be his children. If we refuse to submit to God, we leave a bad taste in the mouth of the world. The world looks at us and says, 'Well, those Christians are no different from us. They respond to affliction just as we do.'

Going to Christ for submission
How do we live, through Christ, the submissive Christian life? Let me quickly give seven suggestions for you to meditate on.

1. Consider Christ's afflictions
Hebrews 12:3 says that if you want to know how to respond to afflictions, consider Christ, meditate on what he has gone through. You will find that you will then no longer have anything to complain about.

2. Consider the power of Christ to deliver and to guide you
Your afflictions are tailor-made by him and fit you better than your best suit of clothes. Believe that!

3. Consider the presence of Christ
'Christ is at no time absent from us.' The Heidelberg Catechism says that so beautifully—'at no time absent'. He is always standing on the shores of our lives as we sail out in all the rough winds and waves. He will never let us go beyond his high-priestly eye; he will never remove us from his high-priestly heart; we are

never beyond the grasp of his high-priestly hands; we are never outside his high-priestly intercessions: 'He ever liveth to make intercession' for us (Hebrews 7:25). And our unbrotherliness to him will never unbrother our precious elder brother from us.

Believe him! Believe that he will take all those waves, and tomorrow's impossibilities that are breaking in on the beachhead of your life, and bring them in a melodious whimper at your feet. They may alarm you, but they will not drown you. He will take care of you—believe that!

4. *Consider the perseverance of Christ*
'Having loved his own which were in the world, he loved them unto the end' (John 13:1). And if he loves his people to the end, he will care for you to the end. From all eternity he has loved you with love unutterable, and he has done too much work on you to let you go.

5. *Consider the prayers of Christ*
His prayers cannot fail. Bring all your prayerlessness to his prayerfulness. His prayers will be answered.

6. *Consider the goals of Christ*
Why does he afflict you? Deuteronomy 8:2 says it is to humble you; Zephaniah 1:12 says it is to teach you what sin is; Hosea 5:15 says that in affliction you will seek God early. Those are all good things, are they not? John Bunyan writes that God's people are like bells: the harder they are hit, the better they sound. Through afflictions God teaches us, says Thomas Watson, to treat the world like a loose tooth in our mouths, which, being easily twitched away, does not much bother us. God ripens us for glory by weaning us from this world.

7. *Consider the end of Christ*
The end of Christ is that you, his bride, may be with him for ever where he is. John Trapp put it this way: 'He that rides to be

crowned will not think much of a rainy day.' You are riding to be crowned, dear child of God, and everything your Father does with you is in order to crown you on the great day.

You know how Persian rugs are made. The rug-maker climbs up some scaffolding and calls down to his rug-workers to pass him all colours of yarn. They hand him up not only the bright colours but also the dark colours, the brown and the black. From beneath they see only a gnarled mass which they do not understand, just as you do not understand why God is dealing with you the way he is.

But one day the rug-maker says, 'Friends, come up higher.' It is said that the rug-workers never fail to be amazed when they climb the ladder, get on to the scaffolding and see the perfect pattern, with all the hues in the right place. Then they understand the skill and wisdom of the rug-maker.

One day God is going to say to you, 'Friend, you whom I have taught to hand up the brown and the black strings, with an amen from your heart, with true submission, you come up higher.' And when we enter the gates of pearly bliss, and behold our lives as a perfect rug, we will see that every string is in the right place. He made no mistakes. We needed just the amount of black yarn he called for. Trust him, and say to him, 'By thy grace it is well with my soul.'

3
The Canaanite woman:
mature faith

(*Matthew 15:21-28*)

We need the *simplicity* of true saving faith, as we have seen in the life of Adam and Eve. We need the *submissiveness* of true saving faith, as we have seen in the life of the Shunammite woman. But we also need great faith, growing faith, mature faith, as we see in the life of the Canaanite woman.

The subject before us—growing faith, mature faith, great faith —is very, very important, and I believe the church needs this faith more than ever before. I am burdened with it for my own life, and I am burdened with it for my brethren and sisters in Christ, for my church, and for the worldwide kingdom of God.

I believe we have a major problem on our hands. We ask people how they became converted—that is well and good, it is wonderful to hear—but all too often the testimony stops after the initial encounter with Jesus Christ. Just as so many people take their husbands or wives for granted once they walk back down the aisle after they are married and still live the way they want to live, far too many Christians stop growing early on in their marriage relationship with the Lord Jesus Christ.

When couples come to me for marital counselling, one of the first questions I ask is, 'Do you really want a better marriage?' I ask that question because many come for help who do not want help. They come because they want self-vindication, or because they want to share with you all that is wrong with their marital partner. So if they say, 'Yes, we really want a better marriage', I say to them, 'How much better? On a scale of 1 to 10, what kind of a marriage do you want? Do you want a 5? Do you want a 7? Do you want a 10? What are you aiming for?' And if they say, 'We want a 10. We want an excellent marriage', then I say, 'I think we can work together. Let's work at it together.'

When I ask, 'On a scale of 1 to 10, what was the best your marriage ever was?', almost inevitably they will reply that it began as a 10. And I will say that no matter how good it was, if they really want a better marriage, then with God's help they can bring it back at least to the point where it once was. So it is, friends, in the spiritual life.

Growing in faith

The great problem of most Christians today is this horrible thing that God hates, that we call backsliding. In this state we take God for granted. We grow stagnant, we settle on our lees and do not grow in grace, we do not fight the spiritual warfare. We listen to sermons, read books and come to conferences, but what we are seeking is self-vindication rather than divine growth and divine conviction. We are not truly yearning to grow in the grace and knowledge of our Lord Jesus Christ. We forget that there are more than three hundred biblical imperatives commanding us to grow in the grace and knowledge of the Lord Jesus Christ.

What would you think of a child who was not growing in maturity? A two-year-old does not want her mother beyond her sight, and you understand; but if a twelve-year-old cannot bear to move away from her mother, you will say, 'There's something wrong. That child is not developing as she should. She has not learned to trust her mother.'

And so it is in spiritual life. We have to learn to walk by faith, and we learn to grow in faith through trials, through absences of God's felt presence, through all the ups and downs of his providential leading in our lives.

The question is, Are you growing in faith? But, you may ask, how do you grow in faith? Well, the Lord has to do that, of course, and he does it by his Spirit, through his Word. But we must be using the Word, we must be begging for the leadings of his Spirit, and we must be yearning for lives that grow and reflect the great blessing of mature faith.

An old minister used to say in our congregation that one mature Christian was worth a hundred immature Christians, because that one person's life would speak. It would make others covet such a life for themselves; it would set a higher tone, a higher level of spirituality, for the congregation and other believers to emulate.

Mature believers help to save us from the bane of easy-believism that permeates and infests the church of our day. And they also foster fellowship in the church. When you see advanced, growing, mature Christians, they are talking about Jesus Christ, they are communing with one another, they are growing in grace. Iron is sharpening iron.

In the Dutch church in days past, there were often fellowships when God's people would meet to talk together about the ways of God and help each other along in their spiritual pilgrimage. And the centre of their conversation would be Jesus Christ and him crucified, and Jesus Christ and him exalted. Oh, how we need such people today!

Fathers and mothers in Israel

So this is my burden. I am so grateful that there are so many new-born Christians, but where are the Aquilas and Priscillas, who are showing the newborns a better way, the way to walk in Christ, the way to live to the glory of God and in the presence of God? Where are those fathers and mothers in Israel?

I am speaking not just of ministers or men, but also of women. What great 'mothers in Israel' there have been in ages past! Many have fed my soul greatly with their spirituality. Think only of the wonderful books that some nineteenth-century women produced. Think of the letters of Ruth Bryan, Sarah Hawkes, Mary Winslow and Ann Dutton. These women were renowned for their godliness, for the maturity of their faith, for the profound levels of communion with God that they reached, and their lives were contagious. We can say of them, as we can say of this Canaanite woman, 'O woman, great is thy faith'.

In my first congregation there was an elderly God-fearing woman who lived to be in her upper nineties. Any minister who came to town went to see her. Everything that dropped from her lips seemed to honour the Lord Jesus Christ, and when you were in her presence you felt you were in the presence of God. She was a woman great in faith. And what a support she was for a minister of the gospel!

I will never forget coming to her one Monday morning. 'How did it go for you yesterday, Pastor?' she asked. 'Well,' I said, 'it was the strangest thing. When I began to preach I was sweating, I couldn't do it, it was all my own work. But halfway through the sermon, the Lord came and took it over for me, and I could hardly keep up with him.' 'Oh,' she said, 'I know, I know. I heard you struggling.' (She was too old to come to church and was at home, listening over the church phone.) 'I turned off the church phone and went into a side room, and I spent the rest of the sermon praying that the Spirit might descend upon you. And I knew he would come. I had contact with God and I knew he would answer my prayer.' 'O woman, great is thy faith.'

Now we are not all going to match this mother in Israel, but if you are a Christian you want your faith to grow, do you not? Do you not want a '10' relationship with the Lord? If we love him, if we are married to him, then why are we settling for such small

61

levels of faith? Why are we taking our Lord for granted? Why are we not striving for greater faith, more maturity, a closer relationship with him? Why are we not putting away this world's shallow, miserable, rotten, stifling entertainment and searching for our Saviour in our Bibles? 'Search the scriptures . . . they are they which testify of me' (John 5:39).

Oh, let us love our Saviour; let us seek to know him better! Let us pray that we may be men and women of faith, whose lives are contagious. Even if others will not look at us and say, 'There's an unusually great person in faith', surely we ought to be growing. Even if we bring forth fruit thirtyfold rather than sixtyfold or a hundredfold, surely we ought to be striving to know our Saviour better.

Well, that is my burden, for myself as well as for others, and I want to share with you from this third biblical portrait three ways in which the Lord Jesus matures a person's faith. He does so, first, by apparent silence (and here we have the first 'but')— 'But he answered her not a word' (verse 23); secondly, by apparent rejection (the second 'but')—'But he answered and said, I am not sent but unto the lost sheep of the house of Israel' (verse 24); and thirdly, by apparent insult (the third 'but')—'But he answered and said, It is not meet to take the children's bread, and to cast it to dogs' (verse 26).

Apparent silence

This is a remarkable story. Consider *how* this woman comes— by true faith, as we shall see; *to whom* she comes—to Jesus himself; *where* she comes—to his very feet; the *urgency* of her coming—crying over and over again, 'Have mercy on me, thou Son of David; my daughter is grievously vexed with a devil'. The Greek indicates repetition; the streets were ringing with her cries. If you consider all this, you would think that surely the Lord Jesus would answer her right away. Has this Canaanite woman not heard in her own land that Jesus hears the cries of beggars, that he heals all who are brought to him, that he gathers little lambs in his arms and carries them in his bosom, and that he will answer before we call? Surely he will be ready to answer this woman immediately, and send her on her way rejoicing.

'But he answered her not a word.' What a contrast: a crying woman and a silent Jesus! What fodder for doubt! Before she left home, people no doubt said to her, 'Why are you going to Jesus of Nazareth? He's the Jewish Messiah. He'll have nothing to do with you, a Canaanite, a foreigner, a Syrophoenician, an outcast.' She has rejected that advice and has come to Jesus—and he answers her not a word.

Now you would think that this woman would return home and say, 'It's no use going to Jesus.' Maybe that would have been your response. Maybe you have done just that. You have gone to him in prayer and turned back.

But this woman does not turn back. Why not? Because true saving faith cannot turn back from God. True saving faith must have God. God is its object. Jesus Christ is the object and the subject. Jesus Christ is the noun and the verb and the adjective and the adverb of true saving faith. He is everything and she cannot do without him. Even silence will not send this woman away.

You, too, have faced the silence of God, have you not? All true Christians who live by faith know at least two things in their spiritual pilgrimage. They know the presence of God, the joy of communion with God, but they also know the sorrow of a silent and an absent God. So often as Christians we act as if God is always at our fingertips and we always have communion with him. But if we are honest, there are many times when we feel the silence of God—and what a burden that silence can be! Samuel Rutherford said that the silence of Jesus Christ is the bitterest ingredient Christians have to drink in their cup of sorrow. He said, 'The silence of my God is hell for my soul.'

Do you know that burden of silence, the burden of a bride who says, 'I will rise now, and go about the city in the streets, and in the broad ways I will seek him whom my soul loveth: I sought him, but I found him not . . . I called him, but he gave me no answer' (Song of Solomon 3:2; 5:6)? Or the cry of Jeremiah, 'When I cry and shout, he [the LORD] shutteth out my prayer . . . Thou hast covered thyself with a cloud, that our prayer should not pass through' (Lamentations 3:8, 44)?

God puts some affliction upon you and you cry to him, but the heavens are as copper and the earth is as desert and you cannot reach him, you cannot gain hold of him. You cannot—as the old Scottish divines used to say—pray until you pray through and lay hold of God. You try to obey him, you try to respond to Isaiah's words when he says to God, 'There is none . . . that stirreth up himself to take hold of thee' (Isaiah 64:7). You cry and shout, you sigh and groan and whisper, but you cannot get beyond the ceiling. Silence, deafening silence! Silence that multiplies the doubts within; silence that influences you to cry out with the psalmist (as we sing from Psalm 42 in our Psalter in America):

> *With anguish as from piercing sword,*
> *Reproach and bitterness I hear;*
> *As day by day with taunting word,*
> *Where is thy God? the scoffers sneer.*

One day, when Martin Luther was leaving his home, he said to his dear wife Katie, 'God is so silent to me, I think he is dead.' That night when he came back from work the shades were drawn, and Luther hastened his step and burst through the door saying, 'Katie, who died?' 'Well,' she said, 'you said this morning that God had died.' And God used that to break Luther's bondage at that particular moment.

Do you not know times when God seems so silent that the doubts are multiplied and you scarcely know how to believe or how to go on? You groan with groanings unutterable (Romans 8:26). God seems to hold himself at bay, and you wonder why. You think of days gone by when he was so close, when he was more real than the chair you are sitting on, for the most real thing in all the world was God. But now he is so far away!

Why does God do that? Why is God sometimes silent to his people? That is a very good question, and, of course, we do not know all the answers to it because we are mere finite people. God is the living, sovereign God, who looks at the entire puzzle of our lives at once. He sees all the thousand pieces of the jigsaw puzzle that make up our lives. We see only one or two pieces at a time, so we never know all the reasons why he acts as he does, and that is proper because God is God. But there are two reasons, two big pieces in the jigsaw puzzle, that we do know; there are two unchanging reasons why God is sometimes so strangely silent in our lives.

For his glory

For the first reason, let me turn you to John 11, where we read that Jesus loved Martha and Mary and Lazarus, and delighted to stay in their home. One day Lazarus becomes very sick, and Martha and Mary send him a message: 'Lord, behold, he whom thou lovest is sick' (verse 3).

Now look at verse 6: 'When he had heard therefore that he [Lazarus] was sick, he abode two days still in the same place where he was.' Does that strike you as strange? If, as soon as I stepped off this podium, I had a call that my wife was sick unto death, I would get on the next plane. I would say, 'It was very wonderful to be here, friends, but I have to go right away. My wife is sick unto death. I love her and I want to be with her.' And you would understand.

How strange! Jesus loves Lazarus, but he stays where he is for two more days. Why? Well, how would Jesus get more glory—through healing a sick Lazarus or through raising a dead Lazarus? And how does Jesus get more glory in our lives? Is it always by coming and answering our prayers right away, or is it by sometimes bringing us to our own wit's end in our prayers, and then answering those prayers when they have been reduced to ashes? From out of the ashes, he revives the flames of hope and faith and love, and gives his answer when we least expect it.

Jesus waited in order to get glory. That is what it says in verse 4: 'This sickness is not unto death'—that is not its purpose—'but for the glory of God, that the Son of God might be glorified thereby.' Think about it this way. If God answered all your prayers right away, who would be given the glory? We would honour ourselves, and our prayerfulness. But God knows how to train us, he knows how to lead us in such a way that 'He that glorieth, let him glory in the Lord' (1 Corinthians 1:31).

To purify our faith

The second reason why God is often silent is to mature, refine and purify our faith. There was once a great nineteenth-century musician who was asked why his playing was so popular and made such an impression, and he said, 'It's the pauses; it's the silences.' Recently a well-known minister attended a service at our church and heard another minister preach. Afterwards he said to me, 'The sermon was all right, it was good, but there wasn't enough white space on the page.'

Have you ever picked up a book that is written from end to end across each double-page spread with no margins? You have to press it right open to read the centre. It is not attractive; there is no white space. You see, we function with white spaces when we read. We function with pauses in our lives. We are wired in such a way that we need pauses, we need reflection, we need times of silence.

In times of silence, God gets us to reflect and to meditate. He brings us into dark tunnels where we can pause and consider his ways. I cannot explain how he does it, but I do know what Peter says: 'that the trial of your faith, being much more precious than of gold that perisheth, though it be tried with fire, might be found unto praise and honour and glory at the appearing of Jesus Christ' (1 Peter 1:7). In dark times in our lives, in times of silence, as God seems to push us away with one hand, with the other hand he is drawing us, silently putting strength in the inner soul. And so somehow, when I come out of that tunnel of affliction and he speaks again with clarity and power in my life, my faith is stronger than it was when I went into that tunnel.

I believe that I have learned more about God in times of his silences than I have in the times when he has not been silent. In times of silence I have learned more about his sovereignty, his holiness, his majesty, and yes, his grace, too. In times of silence I have learned the wonder that I am not destroyed. In times of silence I reflect on God, and then I reflect on myself.

Our text does not say that Jesus did not *hear* a word, but that he did not *answer* a word. Our problem when God is silent is that we think he does not hear us. But he does hear us; he is waiting to be gracious, and he is guiding even silences to his own glory, as we have seen, and to our spiritual maturation.

Dealing with the parent

So Jesus begins to teach this Canaanite woman. Her problem is that she has come to Jesus about her daughter. Have you ever noticed in the Gospels that when someone comes to Jesus about one of his or her children, he always has a way of arresting that person's attention—be it the father of the demoniac, or this woman, or others, too—by dealing with the parent? The woman says, 'My daughter is demon-possessed. Help my daughter, Lord.' But Jesus is silent. He is beginning to work with the woman, with the mother. That is so important.

I have often thought that one of the reasons why God gives us children is to deal with *us*. Thank God, we may not have demon-possessed children, but where is the parent who can raise a child rightly? Have you ever met any parent who says, 'I know how to do it'? The only person who knows how to do it is the one who has not yet had a child! And so God empties us of ourselves and gives us times of silence, even in our parenting, until we begin to reflect upon who we are. And when we see the sins of our children mirroring our own infirmities and sins, in those silences we learn a great deal.

So God begins to deal with this woman. She has come with true saving faith. 'O Lord, thou Son of David'—she has the Messianic title 'Son of David' on her lips. She has some knowledge; the Holy Spirit has taught her something about the Lord Jesus Christ and who he is. That is wonderful. But Jesus says: I want to deal with you now, woman. I want your faith to grow; and I will begin to mature your faith through this reflective silence.

Apparent rejection

Then, secondly, Jesus goes on to mature the woman in two surprising ways: rejection by the apostles, and apparent rejection by Jesus himself.

We read, 'And his disciples came and besought him, saying, Send her away; for she crieth after us' (verse 23). What miserable disciples they were in this case! Terrible pastors, selfish, proud, not discerning. First of all, the woman was not crying after the disciples; she was crying after Jesus. But they were so self-centred that they thought she was crying after them. How dreadfully easy it is for ministers to become self-centred and to forget who people are really crying after when they come for help. And what a powerful example of indifference!

Of course, it may be argued on their behalf that Jesus and the disciples have just come from Galilee to Tyre (a city in Phoenicia, north-west of Galilee) in search of peace and privacy (Mark 7:24), hoping to avoid being arrested, and now here is this woman filling the streets with the noise of her crying. But the bottom line is this: these men are being selfish and indifferent; they do not care for this woman's soul.

Learning to lean on God alone

But my question is, Why would Jesus let his disciples treat the woman in this way? She is just a poor babe in grace, and here she gets this rigorous treatment of rejection. Again, I cannot tell you all the reasons why, but at least I know one piece of the jigsaw puzzle. God has to teach this woman to lose all dependency on people, even ministers, so that she may learn to lean upon Jesus alone. That is growth in faith.

When I was converted, I woke my dad up in the middle of the night—three o'clock in the morning—to tell him what had happened. I told him everything; I told him with tears flowing, unveiling my whole heart and making myself totally vulnerable to him. And my dad's response was to say, 'I only know of a few people in the whole church who've had experiences like that, and they are much older than you.'

It was like a cold shower; he did not believe me. My own God-fearing dad! For two weeks I was in great confusion of mind, and then I read a statement of an old divine, who said that when we are converted, often those closest to us reject us so that we learn to lean on God alone. Then I had my answer—and it is a lesson I have had to learn many times in my life.

So this Canaanite woman is being taught, even through the rejection of the disciples.

But there seems to be a second rejection here. 'Well,' you say, 'the rejection by the disciples is obvious. I can understand that. But why does Jesus seem to reject her?' In verse 24 we have the second 'but': 'But he answered and said, I am not sent but unto the lost sheep of the house of Israel.' Here is a woman crying and begging, and Jesus seems to push her away. Is that not mysterious? You *are* lost, he says; at least you have *that* qualification, but you are not a sheep and you are not of the house of Israel.

Well, how do we understand this? I think Calvin has it right. He says something like this: Christ's priestly work as promised Seed and Saviour, in whom all nations will be blessed, must be distinguished from his prophetical work during his ministry on earth, which was primarily confined to the Jews. The day would come, of course, when he would suffer and die and be raised again and ascend into heaven and send forth his Spirit to break down the middle wall of partition between Jew and Gentile, and Peter and the apostles would bring the prophetical message of Jesus to all people. But that time was not yet. Calvin says that it is as if Jesus is warning her that she is acting out of turn by trying to raid the table in the middle of the supper.

To be rejected by people is hard, but if you are a true Christian, to be rejected by the Lord is harder. To be set outside is a tremendous problem. Do you remember how Rahab, when the young men came to deliver her from Jericho, was left outside the camp of Israel (Joshua 6:23)? What a difficult problem! But then, two verses later, we read that she was brought in: 'She dwelleth in Israel even to this day.'

God can use that experience of being unworthy to be in God's presence, of being fit to be cast away, of being rejected, to mature faith, so that faith casts itself in dependency upon the Lord alone. And that is what happens to this woman. You would think that she would go home now; she is not of the house of Israel; it is as plain as day. Woman, return to your home! But no! We read,

'Then'—just when she is rejected—'came she and worshipped him, saying, Lord, help me' (verse 25). Then she comes, and she falls at his feet. This is the nature of faith. Faith falls unconditionally at God's feet. Faith prays on and pleads on when it seems there is no answer and no solution.

'Lord, help me'

And when faith wrestles with God, more often than not it uses the most simple of prayers. Sometimes our shortest and simplest prayers are our very best: 'Lord, help me.' A two-year-old can pray that prayer, and yet everything is in it. Notice the difference between the woman's first prayer, 'O Lord, thou son of David; my daughter is grievously vexed with a devil', and her second, 'Lord, help me.' There is not one word about her daughter in her second prayer. Did she care less about her daughter? Of course not! But now God is dealing with her. When God deals with me, even if I am worshipping in a large congregation, it seems that God is speaking to me alone, and I learn to cry even in the midst of a crowd, 'Lord, help me.'

In that second prayer the Messianic title 'Son of David' is dropped. Now the woman says, 'Lord'. She appeals to Christ as Lord of heaven and earth, as that great High Priest over all nations. She does not understand all the theology, but the principle is there, none the less: 'Lord, art thou not Lord of heaven and earth? Art thou not Lord beyond the boundaries of Israel? Lord, help me.'

I like to compare this little prayer to a golden necklace. You know, of course, how each link in a necklace connects with the next. Well, here you have a three-word-linkage prayer. You have the little word 'Lord', reaching up into the heavens to the Lord of lords and King of kings, who is Jesus. And you get the word 'me', dropping down into the hell of my own unworthiness. And in the middle is the word 'help': it links into the Lord, because the Lord is our helper in the Lord Jesus Christ, and it reaches down to me. To quote Samuel Rutherford again, 'My Lord is my helper who reaches down into the very bottom of hell, and from the very bottom dregs of hell he links into my soul and lifts me up. His name is Help.'

Do you remember, in John Bunyan's *The Pilgrim's Progress*, how Christian was lifted out of the Slough of Despond by a character named 'Help'? Bunyan says in the margin, '"Help" is Jesus.'

'Lord, help me. I cannot let thee go, Lord. I need thee. I must have thee. I cannot do without thee.' Do you know what it means to pray like that? 'Lord, help me.' It is personal. It is real, urgent, short, and prayed with all your heart.

Worship

We know that the Canaanite woman prayed with all her heart, because verse 25 tells us that she *worshipped* him: 'Then came she and worshipped, saying, Lord, help me.' The word 'worship' is a beautiful word. The Greek word *proskuneo* is formed from two words, *pros* meaning 'toward' and *kuneo* 'to kiss'—'to kiss toward'. The idea is that in worship my mind and my affections are merged together, and go out toward the object of worship.

The Canaanite woman's whole being is centred on Jesus, the same Jesus who seems to reject her. She worships him in the face of rejection. It is as if she says, 'Lord, I'd rather die worshipping at thy feet than live away from thee. Give me Jesus, else I die!' Do you understand that language? Lord, take anything away from me, but do not take Jesus away. I need him. He is my Saviour, my Lord, my Friend, my Kinsman, my elder Brother. There are 280 titles and names for Christ in the Bible, and he is all of them to a believer.

'She . . . worshipped, saying, Lord, help me.' You see, she is growing—growing in faith.

Apparent insult

'Well,' you are going to say, 'the Lord *will* help her now.' But there is one more test, one more sifting, one more purifying process, one more 'but': 'But he answered and said, It is not meet [fitting, proper] to take the children's bread, and to cast it to dogs' (verse 26).

Perhaps you say, 'This is the worst of all!'—because you know that in Bible times most dogs were wild, and to call someone a dog was like calling someone a pig. To call someone a pig or some other beast is very unchristian. Is this our Saviour saying to this woman that it is not meet to take children's bread and throw it to dogs? What is Jesus doing here?

Well, this woman has already confronted and accepted her unworthiness, but now Jesus is dealing with her uncleanness. He is maturing her faith. You see, when God matures our faith, one thing that faith does is to show us that there is nothing in us. William Gurnall put it this way: 'Faith is a two-handed thing. With one hand it takes everything of what I am and wipes it out of the way, and with the other hand it reaches out and takes everything that Christ is and draws it to the soul.'

And that is what faith is doing here for this woman. The Lord Jesus is stripping her down. She is unworthy: she is a Syrophoenician, a Canaanite, a Gentile; she has no natural rights, no religious rights, no citizenship rights. But now the Lord wants to teach her that she is unclean and vile as well as unworthy. She is a sinner, a wretched sinner. The Lord wants to teach her that she is in herself but a filthy dog. He is not aiming at cruelty here; he is maturing her faith.

Faith fighting

How will this woman respond? Will she speak as Abner did in the Old Testament, 'Am I a dog's head?' (2 Samuel 3:8), and angrily walk away? No. She replied, 'Truth, Lord [I am a dog],

73

yet . . .' Luther said that here she gave Christ a master stroke, ensnaring him in his own words—and he was willing to be ensnared. 'But give me, then, if I am a dog, a dog's portion. I don't ask for the children's bread. I don't ask to sit around the table and have a whole loaf. A few crumbs will do, Lord, and if an earthly master will slip a few crumbs off his table, a few of the leftovers, to the dogs under the table, certainly thou, who art a loving master, wilt slip a few crumbs over the edge of the table of Israel into this Canaanitish heart.'

What a beautiful stretch of faith this woman exercises here! This is the way to wrestle with God. She is a New Testament Jacob, saying, 'I will not let thee go, except thou bless me' (Genesis 32:26). 'Truth, Lord: yet . . .' I say it with the utmost reverence, but this woman here is engaging in holy argumentation with the Saviour.

There is such a thing as a holy argument with God. Job came to that place when the Lord was maturing his faith through his troubles. He said, 'Oh that I knew where I might find him!' (Job 23:3), and then adds, 'I would order my cause before him, and fill my mouth with arguments' (verse 4). This is a holy wrestling with the Lord. We need to know more of that today; we need more of that maturity. We need more who will say, like Asaph, 'I was as a beast before thee' (Psalm 73:22), and with David, 'LORD, be merciful unto me' (Psalm 41:4, 10, etc.), and Paul, 'sinners; of whom I am chief. Howbeit . . . I obtained mercy' (1 Timothy 1:15, 16).

Taking God at his word

So how do you do it? You take God at his word. That is what this woman did. In the New King James Version, 'dogs' is translated as 'little dogs', and that is a good translation. Though in Old Testament times all dogs were wild, by the time of the New Testament, people were beginning to bring smaller dogs into the home as pets, and those dogs would sit under the table. So the woman takes up that word 'little dogs', sticks her beggar's foot in the door and says, 'Lord, thou hast called me a little dog; well, let me be a little dog under thy table and give me the portion of goods that falls to me. Let me take thee at thy word.'

How do you do that today? William Gurnall said: You take the promises of God, and in prayer you turn them inside out and bring them back to God again. You take the promise and turn it into a petition. 'The Lord is my shepherd; I shall not want': O Lord, art thou not my Shepherd? Lord, fill me with everything I need. 'He maketh me to lie down in green pastures: he leadeth me beside the still waters': Lord, lead me into thy Word.

Another Puritan said, 'God is tender of his own handwriting. He loves to read his own letters to you. Show him his hand-writing.' I have often noticed that in those old books of prayers of ministers of ages past, many of the prayers are almost nothing but a string of texts put together in a new order. In text after text they are bringing God his own word. That is the way to argue with God.

Truth, Lord: yet . . .
—I am blind, but hast thou not eyesight for the blind?
—I am poor, but hast thou who wast rich not become poor, that poor sinners may be made rich in thee?
—I am weak, but art thou not the strong one?
—I am unrighteous, but art thou not the LORD our Righteousness?
—I am a dog, but dost thou not have crumbs for dogs?

Keeping your foot in the door

When my dad was nine years old, a beggar came to the door one day. My grandfather was an immigrant and my grandparents were very poor. They lived in a very little home with just a few rooms. They ate mostly from the garden. The beggar said to my dad, 'Can I have a sandwich?' My dad went to my grandmother and said, 'There's a beggar at the door and he wants a sandwich.' And my grandmother said, 'You go back to the beggar and tell him we're just as poor as he is.'

So my dad went back and said to the beggar, 'We're just as poor as you are. We cannot give you a sandwich.' He tried to close the door but could not because the beggar had stuck his foot in it. He looked up at the beggar, and the beggar looked down at him and said, 'One slice of bread.' Not knowing what to do he went back to my grandma and said, 'The beggar won't go away. He wants one slice of bread.' 'Oh,' said my grandmother, 'he's a real beggar. Give him a whole sandwich!'

That is what God does with spiritual beggars. He tests our authenticity. In my first congregation, I also had a beggar at my door, and I began to question what he would do with the money that I was prepared to give him. He said, 'What is your business what I do with that money?' And he turned round and walked away. How much did he get? Nothing, of course.

High on John Bunyan's list of sins—where he confesses his shortcomings before God—is this: 'My problem is I knock at the door of grace but once or twice, and then leave the Lord alone.' How do you feel when a salesman knocks on your door and you go and answer it, only to find that by then he is halfway through the neighbourhood? Do you call after him, or do you close the door and say, 'Well, he didn't want me very badly, he only knocked once'?

The beggar sticks his foot in the door. Do you have an un-converted child, a wandering prodigal, for whom you have been praying for two or three years? Keep your foot in the door! God is maturing your faith through that beggary. Do you know what would happen if all your children were beautiful, wonderful, strong Christians, stalwart sons and daughters of Jesus Christ in the faith? You would be a proud dad. God is maturing you through your children. Keep that beggar's foot in the door. Show God his priorities. Show him his covenant faithfulness. 'Truth, Lord'—my son is wandering far away and I cannot reach him. 'Truth, Lord'—he was converted, but I was a bad father. 'Truth, Lord'—I made so many mistakes. Yet art thou not the God of the covenant? Bring back this child, Lord! Bring back this child!

I come from a paedo-baptist tradition, and I am not trying to push infant baptism here, but I want to tell you a short story. My father and mother had a very difficult time with one of my sisters for a little while. When she was seventeen years old she left home, and for three weeks they had no idea where she was. You can imagine how they prayed.

One day my dad was going by the church and he went in (he was an elder for many years and had a key). He went to the very spot where she had been baptised as a baby. (You may think this sounds mystical, but he did not do it mystically.) He fell on his face at that spot and said, 'O God of the covenant, God who hast promised to take from our seed, and our seed's seed, and to draw them to thyself, O God, hear our cry. Truth, Lord, I am an unworthy father, but have mercy upon our child. Was she not named with thy name as she was baptised? Was she not baptised in the name of the Father and of the Son and of the Holy Ghost? O God, confirm thine own name.'

So he wrestled. When he got home, my mother met him at the door, weeping. She said, 'Our daughter just called.' He said, 'When?' It had been the very time that he was wrestling on that church floor. He called her up and she said, 'I want to come home, Dad. Am I still welcome?' It was the beginning of her con- version.

God can use the greatest obstacles, the greatest burdens. God used this demon-possessed daughter to cause the mother to grow in grace. And every problem you have, my dear Christian friends, whether it be with a child or because of an illness, whatever it may be in your life, that affliction is designed by God to mature you in the faith, so that you become a wrestler with God, and a beggar who sticks a foot in the door at the throne of grace. You keep your foot there! God is maturing you through every single trial.

So what do we see in this woman? We see what we talked about right at the beginning. We see the three great acts of faith. She had saving knowledge: 'O Lord, thou son of David'. She had saving assent: 'Truth, Lord: yet the dogs eat of the crumbs which fall from their master's table.' And she had trust: 'Then came she and worshipped him.' She put all her marbles in one basket: 'Lord, help me. Lord, it is either thee or I perish.' That is trust.

This woman puts us all to shame. She was just like Adam and Eve, you remember, who knew so little about Jesus, yet believed. She knew so little about Jesus; she was a foreigner; she was not in church every week—and yet she believed and trusted and persevered, and she gained the victory.

God's giving

Finally, Jesus answers the Canaanite woman, 'O woman, great is thy faith' (verse 28). Do you notice how he calls it 'thy faith'? It was really the faith he had given to her. He did all the exercising of faith within her, and yet what he gives away is '*thy* faith'. It is like what happens when I have a birthday. I give money to my wife to give money to my child to go out and get a present for me, and the child comes and gives me the present and I say, 'Thank you for your gift'!

We bring back to God what he gives to us, and God takes such delight in his own work in his own people that he says, 'It is really yours, and whatever I give to you I give away to you.' God is no indigent, miserly giver. He gives everything. He gave the best he had—his Son—for the worst he could find—sinners like you and me. He gives it all.

And so he gives to this woman (may I say it this way?) two loaves of bread, not crumbs. He sends her away to her daughter, and her daughter is at once made whole. She was healed the very moment Jesus spoke. Imagine! The daughter is in her right mind, free of demon-possession; and the first thing they talk about, I should think, is Jesus, the wonderful Saviour. The daughter is wondrously healed. It is as if Jesus says, 'Woman, here are the keys to my storehouse. You can go and have what you want.' The text says, 'O woman, great is thy faith: be it unto thee even as thou wilt.'

Why did Jesus trust her? Why did he trust her to take anything she wanted? Because it was his work in her, and he knew that what she wanted most of all was Jesus himself. When we want Jesus himself most of all, the Lord gives everything to us. In his time and in his way, he says, 'Be it unto thee even as thou wilt.' If you wait on God, you will never, never be disappointed.

Serve the Lord!

Young people, Satan, I know, is trying to whisper in your hearts that it is not worthwhile to serve the Lord. I say to you that it is *only* worthwhile to serve the Lord; it is never worthwhile to serve this poor, perishing, wicked world.

This morning, while I was meditating on a bench on the promenade, an old gentleman met me. He told me he was ninety years old and said, 'I was saved when I was twenty—seventy years ago. I just can't understand what anyone can see in this world. I love the Bible; I devour the Bible.' (I just love that expression, 'I devour the Bible'—after seventy years!) 'I taught myself Hebrew and Greek', he said, 'when I was fifty years old, and I love the Bible and search it every day.'

To serve the Lord is the most exciting thing of all. You will not get crumbs when you serve the Lord; you will get full loaves of bread. The world will give you crumbs, filthy, polluted crumbs, poisonous crumbs that will spoil you and make you sick and bring you to hell. Do not follow this world. It is so empty, so terribly empty. Follow the Lord!

Perhaps you have heard that wonderful story about Richard Cecil, a contemporary of John Newton. Richard Cecil was very discouraged: he was preaching and preaching, but, as is the experience of many preachers, the people did not put into practice what he was saying. One day, sitting in his study feeling very downhearted, he looked out of the window and saw a pig-farmer going to market. Surprisingly, all the pigs were following the farmer like faithful disciples, walking right behind him to the slaughterhouse. So he followed the pig-farmer, wanting to know how he did it.

When the pig-farmer came out of the slaughterhouse, Richard Cecil asked him, 'How do you get pigs to follow you to their own deaths, when I cannot get people to follow me to their eternal life?' 'Oh,' said the pig-farmer, 'didn't you see what I had in my pockets? As I walked along, now and then I just dropped a few crumbs of this pig-food. The pigs were so hungry even for a few crumbs that they followed me right to their slaughter.'

My friends, I ask you, whoever you are, young and old, will you destroy your life for the poor pig-food of the prodigal son, for a few crumbs of it? Will you follow Satan, who drops it in your pathway, even to the slaughterhouse of everlasting dereliction and hell? Will you not turn from your evil ways and repent and live and believe the gospel and become a beggar? Oh, there is greater joy in being a non-possessing beggar at the foot of the throne of grace than there is in being a possessing worldling with the whole world at your feet.

'What shall it profit a man, if he shall gain the whole world, and lose his own soul?' (Mark 8:36). You are going to eternity, and you have one soul to gain or lose. Let me quote Rutherford once more. He said, 'If you had a thousand souls, you could not

80

afford to give up one of them to the world. I would want my Saviour to have all thousand of them.' Why risk your one soul?

The real silence, rejection and insult

But maybe you have one closing question. This woman was unworthy. She was a sinner. How could Jesus bestow all these wonderful blessings upon this heathen Canaanitish woman?

Well, the answer is because of Christ himself. How did Christ teach her through his apparent silence? Because he faced the *real silence* before his own Father. He faced the closed heaven. He was not pushed away with one hand and drawn with the other; he was pushed away with both hands. He cried out in the most awesome, deafening silence the world has ever known, 'My God, my God, why hast thou forsaken me?' (Matthew 27:46).

He went through that so that you, as a believer, might never face anything more than *apparent* silence. You may face the shadow of silence at times, but he endured the substance of it for your sake. And so he shall not be silent for ever. David's prayer will be answered: 'Be not silent to me: lest, if thou be silent to me, I become like them that go down into the pit' (Psalm 28:1). That will never happen, because Jesus Christ went down into the pit under the silent hand of the heavenly Father.

Jesus Christ also faced the *real rejection*. He was thrust away by his Father in heaven; thrust away by his disciples; thrust away by the very realm of nature—the sun would not shine upon him. He was thrust away by the demons of hell; he hung between earth and heaven. It was total rejection.

And he was *insulted* as no man ever was. He was called something worse than a dog; he was called Beelzebub, the prince of the devils. He was mocked, spat upon, taunted: 'If thou be Christ, save thyself and us' (Luke 23:39). And he could have come down from that cross in a moment. He could have vindicated himself. He could have destroyed all those around the cross. He could have shown his power. But he stayed on that cross to go on being insulted, so that he could take your place, so that all your insults could only be shadows, and he could bear the substance for you.

Jesus Christ is never really silent to his people, and he never rejects them, and he never insults them. But he uses these apparent things to lead you to himself, and to mature your faith, so that you will grow in communion with him, with whom you are in union by faith. 'Lord, increase our faith!'

4
Caleb:
persevering faith

(*Numbers 13:25–14:24*)

If we are to keep going in the Christian life, we need not only the simple, childlike faith of Adam and Eve, the submissive faith of the Shunammite woman, and the growing and maturing faith of the Canaanite woman, but we also need the persevering, following and wholehearted faith of Caleb, this great man of God, who persevered for eighty-five years in the midst of murmuring Israelites.

The miracle of perseverance

I sometimes think that the persevering dimension of the Christian life is the greatest miracle of all. When we preach on Pentecost from Acts 2:4 about how the Holy Spirit filled the house where the apostles were sitting, and gave them utterance so that they could speak and preach to the people in their own languages, we are awed by the miraculous character of the outpouring of the Spirit. But perhaps a later verse is every bit as miraculous. In Acts 2:42 we read these words: 'And they continued stedfastly in the apostles' doctrine and fellowship, and in breaking of bread, and in prayers.'

It is a wonder to become a Christian, but it is also a wonder to *remain* a Christian. When you consider what we are in ourselves, sometimes the greater wonder is that the Lord keeps us converted, that he allows us to persevere, that he does not abandon us; because now when we sin, we sin against the cross, against the blood, and against his love. What a wonderful thing perseverance is!

A word to ministers

And may I say to my fellow brethren in the ministry, you will be helped to persevere in the gospel in this day of small things, if you reckon with the reality that all around us are people who are submerged in worldly things. Out of 168 hours a week, they have perhaps 3 hours in the house of God. When you do not see much progress, consider the miracle that God uses, basically, those three hours and a few daily devotions, to retain these people even at their present level of spirituality, in the face of a powerful, terrorising, godless world that bombards them for most of the other hours of the week with its philosophy. Sometimes that thought helps me when I say, 'Where's the progress of those young saints?' I think of what a wonder it is that they are not backsliding; at least they are holding their own. It is a wonder that the Word does even that.

But we want more than that, do we not? We want to grow, we want our people to grow, we want to persevere in the most holy faith. We need as ministers, first of all, to show our people examples of that kind of perseverance. Could it be that God has put you in a small charge in a day of small things, and has shown you but small fruits, in order that you may stand as a beacon and example for your people and to the world around you, as a faithful minister of the gospel who is emulating and modelling the grace of our God in the Lord Jesus Christ? Could it be that God has withheld showing you great fruits in your ministry, so that you might be a living example of those who keep their hand on the plough and do not look back? For 'No man, having put his hand to the plough, and looking back, is fit for the kingdom of

God' (Luke 9:62). Brethren, labour on: 'Cast thy bread upon the waters: for thou shalt find it after many days' (Ecclesiastes 11:1)—if not in this life, then on the Great Day.

Samuel Rutherford said, 'Heaven will be two heavens to me when I meet one other soul from Anworth there.' So will it be for you when you meet your own people, on the day of judgement, on the right hand of the great Shepherd of the sheep. Even if you were used for one soul, all the labour expended would be well worth it, to spend eternity with that person praising and glorifying the Lamb.

Following God fully

But every one of us needs mentors in this regard, and I want to set before you Caleb, a great man of God who, in times every bit as bad and even worse than ours, and against all human odds, persevered in consistent and persistent and fulsome faith. And so I want to preach to you from Numbers 14:24:

> But my servant Caleb, because he had another spirit with him, and hath followed me fully, him will I bring into the land whereinto he went; and his seed shall possess it.

My theme is 'Persevering in faith by following God fully', and with God's help I want to pursue three main thoughts. First, what it means to follow God fully; secondly, its root—why and how Caleb could follow God fully; and thirdly, the reward God gives upon following God fully.

On the day I was ordained into the ministry, my father shook my hand and said to me, 'Son, today you have finally begun. But remember, it will be harder to persevere than to begin, but the grace of God will be sufficient for both if you stay close by him.' That is what is so remarkable about Caleb. Of course he was a sinner, of course he was a man of like passions as we are, but you never read that he ever strayed from God. He is an amazing example. God says of him—I am sure Caleb would not have said it about himself because he would have known his own heart—'[he] hath followed me fully'. It is wonderful when other saints can say that of us, but it is amazing when God can say it.

You remember what God said of Job: he was 'a perfect and an upright man' (Job 1:8; 2:3). God did not mean that Job never sinned, but that he was following him fully. Job did not say that of himself, did he? But God said it of him, and God says it of Caleb. Persevering faith. Fulsome faith. That is what we need, friends, by the grace of God.

The spies

Now who was this Caleb? You know, of course, that Caleb was one of the twelve spies sent out by Moses with God's permission to search the promised land. One was sent from every tribe. Israel was encamped at Kadesh-barnea on the edge of the desert, on the border of the promised land, ready to do battle against its inhabitants, ready to conquer them as God had promised.

After forty days these twelve spies returned. Remarkably, all twelve of them agreed on the basic objective facts. They all agreed that the land of Canaan was a good land, a land that flowed with milk and honey. They even brought back a huge cluster of grapes from Eshcol as proof. They all agreed that the inhabitants of this land were, for the most part, a warlike people, and that there were giants, 'the sons of Anak', who would be a fearsome foe. And they agreed that the cities were strongholds surrounded by strong bulwarks. They all agreed that it would be complicated and difficult to fight the Canaanites.

The majority report

But when it comes to interpreting these facts, the spies have a division among them. There is a majority report turned in by ten out of the twelve, and that report is very negative. It says, 'We be not able to go up against the people; for they are stronger than we' (Numbers 13:31). That is the conclusion. 'It's as plain as day that it's no use going forward. We're outnumbered.'

The majority decision was dictated by reasoning and unbelief. Fear and unbelief were the parents of their conclusions. They had the facts straight, but they had the conclusion wrong because they had omitted the greatest fact of all, the fact of God and his promise—the God of the Red Sea; the God of the wonders of ages past; the God who had said, 'Canaan, which I give unto the children of Israel' (Numbers 13:2).

Unbelief, the antonym of faith, is such a deadly foe because unbelief reasons with flesh and blood. Unbelief tallies up the size of the walls and the giants and the Amalekites and the Canaanites, and unbelief concludes that it is impossible to go forward. The outcome of this tragic story was that the people sided with the majority report, and these ten men were responsible for leading two and a half million Israelites into the Slough of Despond in unbelief. What a tragedy!

What a calling ministers have! In some ways it is the calling of a spy. Every week we go out and spy through the Scriptures, and on the coming Sabbath we bring back to our people a report of the land—a report of God and his promises, a report of the heavenly land of Canaan, a report of how to traverse the earthly land by faith. Woe be to us if we bring to our people a message of unbelief, a message of hopelessness, a message in which God is left out of the equation!

What a cruel report these spies brought back! Here they come, carrying on a pole a huge cluster of grapes from the Valley of Eshcol. Then, laying the grapes before the people, they say, 'Look at these wonderful grapes from this wonderful land! But you can't have them, because we're not going in. You can see it, but you can't have it. It's no use.' That is torture.

Have you ever tried that with a child? Imagine bringing home a beautiful new bike and saying, 'Look at this wonderful bike. It's a great bike. Walk around it. Isn't it great? But you can't have it!'

You can preach the gospel in that way. You can make it great; you can talk about the wonderful blessings of the gospel. But if you do not show sinners the way, and fail to encourage them in that way, and do not tell them to go in by faith, you are like the ten false spies.

The minority report

Well, happily there are two other spies. They come, believing what even unbelieving Balaam would have to say from a donkey: 'God is not a man, that he should lie; neither the son of man, that he should repent: hath he said, and shall he not do it? or hath he spoken, and shall he not make it good?' (Numbers 23:19).

Caleb stands up, quiets all the people, and says exactly what they do not want to hear. They really want to hear that they cannot go into the land, because they are afraid, they are unbelieving. He says, 'Let us go up at once, and possess it; for we are well able [by the strength of our God] to overcome it' (Numbers 13:30); 'They [the people] are bread for us . . . and the LORD is with us: fear them not' (14:9). You see, with God all things are possible, and with God a minority gains the victory.

I had a ministerial friend in Nigeria who was discouraged in his ministry in a remote and lonely part of the country. The numbers were very few, everything was going down, and he was saying to himself, 'Why am I here? What hope is there?' And one day, in God's providence, a little old run-down rickety truck went bouncing along in front of his home through all the bumps and potholes of the street. He looked at that truck in amazement: on the side of it, in crude red letters, was painted, 'God plus one equals majority.'

Caleb really believed that, and therefore he had the courage to stand up and face all those hundreds of thousands of people and say, 'Let us go up at once.' He did not say, 'Oh, well, we spies disagree, so we'll now discuss this problem among ourselves. We'll have a conference and come back to you in about four days. We'll see if we can come up with a compromise position.' No, God had spoken; God had promised. 'Lord, do as thou hast said!'

There are many things in our lives that we do not need to pray about. Perhaps you have never thought about it that way. You do not have to pray about discerning God's will in areas where God has already made his will known. God had made his will known about going into Canaan. It was plain and clear; they had to go in at once. But when we do not want to do God's will, what we so often do in our pious Christian way is to say, 'Well, I'll pray about it.' Those prayers are an abomination to God, because his will is known.

Those who persist in low levels of obedience will persist in false petitions, and they will persist in low levels of assurance as well. God has connected together obedience and his Word. When he speaks, it is to be done. It is not to be postponed until tomorrow. Tomorrow's faith is simply today's unbelief. 'Let us go up at once', said Caleb; the people are given to us because God has promised.

So all the spies saw the same facts, but Joshua and Caleb had a heart for God, a heart for his promise, and a heart for the people. They saw the same things with their eyes, but reached different conclusions from the heart. What a difference this makes! Unbelief is always dreadfully contagious: it persuades people that the giants of Anak are larger than the promises of God; it makes God look small and giants look big; it eats away at the vitals of faith; it stunts spiritual growth. Is that not true? Every time you are unbelieving in the presence of God, your spiritual

. ...ı is bruised and stunted. But true faith, persevering faith, turns the giants into dwarves, and shows God to be big, as he really is.

Persevering faith is realistic faith. I do not say that persevering faith is *easy* faith, but I do say that persevering faith is *sure* faith. There is a sure way when saved sinners persevere with God, believing his promises, trusting in his Word. They may go through difficult times in furnaces of affliction, through tunnels of challenges, but God will bring them out. Proverbs 23:18 says, 'For surely there is an end; and thine expectation shall not be cut off.' God is always true to his Word. He always meets, or even exceeds, his promises. He does 'exceeding abundantly above all that we ask or think' (Ephesians 3:20). This minority believes in God and, believing in God, they come with a positive report: Let us go in and take the land!

Faith under scrutiny

Now may I ask you, my friend, does your life display a positive report of God based on God's promises, or a negative report of your own complaints and your own unbelief? It is not only unbelief that is contagious; true faith is contagious, too. Your life is contagious for good or for ill. People are watching you, especially when you claim to be a Christian. They are watching you carefully, far more than you may realise, watching every move you make.

When I was in the army, the drill sergeant said to us—it is part of the harassment of the army!—that we could only have two pairs of boots. We had to have white dots on the backs of one pair of boots, and we had to wear the white-dot boots and the non-white-dot boots on alternate days. You could not disobey. The point was, of course, that every night you had to polish the boots you had to wear the following day. So every night you had to keep up with all this polishing.

Well, I did not like polishing my boots every night, so—yes, I bought a third pair of boots! And I had that third pair of boots in my locker. One day, I opened up my locker and my room partner (who was not a Christian) saw them. 'I've something to ask you', he said; 'Why do you have three pairs of boots?' 'Well,' I replied, 'I got myself a third pair of boots because I don't like polishing very much.' 'But the drill sergeant said you should only have two pairs.' 'Yes, but you know . . .' Then, looking me straight in the face (I will never forget; it is thirty years later now, but I remember his face vividly), he said, 'I thought you were a Christian!'

The world will notice the smallest inconsistency. But the good news is that the world will also notice if you are consistent. People will begin to feel that there is something in your life that is missing from theirs, and they will ask you questions. They will test you. Is this minority report for real, or is it a sham? Is Christianity really vital? Is it really true? What do people see when they look at your life? Are you a Caleb, walking consistently with your God? Are you following God fully?

You perhaps know the story of an old Puritan, Richard Rogers, who was once challenged by a gentleman who said, 'Mr Rogers, I like you and your company very well, only you are too precise.' 'Oh, sir,' said Rogers, 'I serve a precise God.' He meant that in a good way, in a loving way. When you walk in a precise way, not a precise legalistic way but a precise way according to God's law, out of love, and people see that love, there will be a certain level of contagiousness in your life. The Heidelberg Catechism says, 'that by our godly conversation others may be gained to Christ.'

What it means to follow fully

Numbers 14:24 is not the only place in the Bible where we are told that Caleb followed God fully. In Joshua 14:13 we read that Joshua speaks to Caleb, blesses him and gives him Hebron 'for an inheritance'. And then verse 14 continues, 'Hebron therefore became the inheritance of Caleb the son of Jephunneh the Kenezite unto this day, because that he wholly followed the LORD God of Israel.' Caleb was then eighty-five years old. He had fully followed God when he was forty; he fully followed God when he was eighty-five. Through forty years in the wilderness, forty years surrounded by murmuring Israelites, forty years of unbelieving, complaining people on every side, he had followed God fully. That is amazing!

It may be that as a Christian you feel very alone, that there are few Christians around you. But here is your encouragement: it is possible to be a Daniel in the courts of Babylon; it is possible to be a Caleb in the midst of a murmuring wilderness people. You can stay faithful to the Lord.

What does it mean, then, to follow God fully? There are a number of things one could say, but let me give you just four of them.

Persistently

Caleb followed God persistently, and I take that to mean that he followed God *evenly*. He did not live his religion, as John Warburton once said, in fits and starts. He lived his religion consistently, day in, day out. He persevered during all those years in the midst of the camp of the murmurers. He was faithful unto death.

There are a lot of people who are religious by fits and starts, are there not? There are the Jews in John 6, who were walking with Jesus but then turned away. There are the Galatians, who began to run well and then backtracked. There is Lot's wife, who left the city but looked back.

There was a young man in my congregation who, when he was very ill in intensive care, said to me, 'Pastor, if the Lord ever brings me out of this hospital, I'll consecrate my whole life to him.' He is now back with his old friends and is as worldly as ever. What a tragedy!

What about you, my friend? Can you join God's people on Sunday and look like a saint, and be a chameleon on Monday and look like the world? Are you following God seven days a week? In the way you talk, do you sound like the world? Can the world hear and see from you that you are coming from another world, a heaven-born world?

I will never forget how, when I was first saved, I so desperately needed communion with God that I went around to all my friends telling them that I could not be their friend temporarily because I had to spend time in the Word. One friend was so puzzled that he said to me, 'You're talking like someone who's coming from another world.' It did not dawn on me until years later that he was right. It *is* another world to be a Christian; it is a whole other world. We do not need to hide it, nor do we need to flaunt it. We need to show genuinely, in a natural way, by our conversation, by our way of life, that we follow the Lord seven days a week, and that we do not belong to this poor, miserable world which is outwardly happy only on weekends. 'Thank God it's Friday!' is what the world says.

In one seminary class that I attended, the lecturer had written on the board 'TGIM'. We saw these letters as we walked in, and we were debating what they could mean when he entered and said, 'Thank God it's Monday.' A Christian, you see, a true, godly Christian, wants to serve God seven days a week. He enjoys his work because his work is an opportunity to serve the living God. Is that your goal? Is that your pursuit? Do you persistently strive to live to the glory of God as Caleb did?

Sincerely

To follow God fully also means to follow him sincerely, with all my heart, and to do this even if there were no heaven and no hell, because God is lovable, and he is worthy to be served and feared and adored. To follow God means to follow him with all my heart in every situation, no matter what people do to me, and no matter what they say about me. In the big things and the little things in life, we must follow God wholeheartedly.

The people picked up stones to stone Caleb (14:10), but he did not flinch. He did not back down. He would rather die than stop following his God. He was willing to endure insults and jeers; he was willing to endure the disfavour of men, so that he might enjoy the favour of God. Caleb had the fear of God in his heart, and how we need that same fear today!

Do you know why Christians are so rarely like salt in the earth? Why have we lost so much of our saltiness? It is because we do not portray, from the inside out, the fear of God. What is the fear of God? The best definition I have ever read is by John Brown, who said, 'The fear of God is to esteem the smiles and frowns of God to be of greater weight and value than the smiles and frowns of men.' Did Caleb care if they stoned him? Of course he cared, but he cared more about the smile of his God.

But this also applies to the small things in life. One example that comes to my mind is a little army story. At lunchtime on the first day I was in the army, I carried my tray to the table and sat down to eat my lunch. I prayed, of course, silently, and when I opened my eyes my tray was gone. There was a whole table full of guys. I looked around but could not find my food. I waited about thirty seconds without saying a word.

Then a guy, two down and across the table, said to me, 'So where did your food go, praying boy?' I said, 'Well, I don't know where it went, but God knows.' He said, 'Do you really believe that God hears you?' 'I *know* God hears me', I said. He was silent for a moment, then one of the other guys said, 'Oh, give it back to him, buddy.' So they gave it back to me.

That is just a tiny example. But even in the smallest details of life, are you willing to speak a word for God, wherever it may be? Why are we so shy? The world is never afraid to speak about its agenda. Why are we so timid about standing up for the name of our God and taking a little ridicule, a little persecution, when our Master took so much for us? Follow God sincerely. Every person you meet who is unconverted is your mission field. View people that way, and pray for opportunities to speak and to walk before them in the ways of God.

Three weeks ago I was in my brother's bookshop in Ontario, Canada, when a man walked in who wanted some Bibles for Turkey. My brother showed him thirty-seven Bibles in a box and said he could have them for $2 each. The man said, 'I'd like to tell you a story about what is going on in Turkey.' This is the story he told.

I have a minister friend in Turkey who was distributing Bibles and got imprisoned. His tormentors said, 'Tell us who gave you those Bibles.' 'I'll never tell you who gave me the Bibles,' he said, 'they are brethren and sisters in the Lord.' 'Well,' they said, 'we will persuade you'; but the man replied, 'Never mind.'

So they took him into a torture chamber and ripped off one of his toenails. When he was in pain, they said, 'Now tell us who gave you the Bibles.' He said, 'I will never tell you.'

They ripped off another toenail, then another, and another. Each time they asked the same question, and each time he gave the same answer. They ripped off ten toenails, but still he would not tell. They asked, 'Why won't you tell?' He said, 'My Master suffered much more than you put me through and he never told against me.' They said, 'Oh, we'll get you to tell, it's just a matter of time.' 'No,' he said, 'I will never tell.'

They ripped off a fingernail, and they went through all ten fingernails. Then they began on his teeth: pulling out one tooth at a time with a pair of pliers, they emptied his entire mouth. And after every single fingernail, every single tooth, they said, 'Tell us.' 'No, I will never tell you', he replied.

Finally, they hung him upside down in that torture room and beat him around the ankles and feet ninety-nine times—the maximum allowed by Islamic law. After every beating they asked him to tell, and each time he refused. They then gave up, picked him up like a sack of potatoes and threw him out into the street, where he lay as a beggar.

But in God's providence, one of the very few Christian missionary women in Turkey happened to walk by and see this beggar in the street. Like the good Samaritan, she had compassion and somehow managed to get the strength to carry him to her home. She nursed him for three months, and was astonished to find out that he, too, was a Christian missionary, and to hear his story. The woman then sent him to Louisiana in America, where he spent six months in a hospital. When he came out of hospital after all that time, he could walk about fifty feet with the aid of two canes.

The church was so impressed with his testimony that they asked him to preach, and then invited him to become their pastor. But he said no. 'Why not?' they said; 'You need to recuperate.' 'No, I have to go back to Turkey', he said. 'Why would you go back to Turkey?' 'I have to distribute more Bibles.'

He went back to Turkey, distributed more Bibles and got imprisoned again. But in God's amazing providence, when the case was taken to court the second time, because he really did not know where the Bibles came from, he was set free.

That man was set free six weeks ago now as we speak, and three weeks ago his friend came into my brother's bookstore for more Bibles. You can imagine my brother's response. He said, 'You take those Bibles for nothing!'

You see, this man has a firm resolve. There is no negotiation. His life is here for only one purpose: he is going to follow God. There is no other agenda. That is what makes for a strong Christian.

That is the determination that Paul had, did he not? He wrote, 'For I determined not to know any thing among you save Jesus Christ, and him crucified' (1 Corinthians 2:2). Paul had a thousand things he could have been engaged in, but he said: No, I am going to control my mind, I am going to control my time. I have one agenda, one goal in life. I am like a horse with blinkers or blinders on. I am living and I am dying for the Lord Jesus Christ.

Paul followed God sincerely, with all his heart. May God help us to do that. It does not mean that people are going to rip out our toenails and fingernails, but in some ways we are going to suffer persecution. You cannot live as a Christian in this world without suffering persecution. Martin Luther said that persecution is an essential mark of the true church. 'All that will live godly in Christ Jesus shall suffer persecution' (2 Timothy 3:12). You cannot follow a reproached Master and not ever be reproached yourself. My friend, you have to be willing to pay the price to be a Christian. You have to follow God by persevering and sincere faith, and God will help you. 'He that loveth father or mother more than me is not worthy of me' (Matthew 10:37).

Indivisibly
The word 'indivisible' is the word used by the old divines. Thomas Boston used the term 'universally'. It means to follow God in the whole panorama of my life, to follow all his commandments, all his will, all his means of grace. It means to say with the psalmist, 'Then shall I not be ashamed, when I have respect unto all thy commandments' (Psalm 119:6), and 'I will run in the way of thy commandments' (Psalm 119:32).

Caleb did not pick and choose. Some people today say, 'I follow nine commandments.' But God gave ten! Other people pick and choose certain areas about which they say, 'It isn't so bad if I do this.' Do you ever hear Christians begin a statement like this: 'I know this isn't right but . . . .'?

Anything that is not right that you knowingly do is going to bring you away from God, and anything you do that brings you away from God is never worth the price. It dampens and injures your spiritual life, and it stunts your faith. As Christians, we have no business following God with a halting, partial obedience. We must obey him fully, not picking and choosing, but asking in all things, 'Lord, what wilt thou have me to do?' (Acts 9:6).

Part of that obedience means being in the Word daily, using the means of grace faithfully. You cannot maintain a strong, vibrant Christian witness without daily communion with God. My friend, you have got to make a resolve that from this day on you will not relegate your daily communion with God to third or fourth place, but will make it number one. 'I must seek the face of God before the face of man every morning', said Robert Murray McCheyne. The only way to live is to serve the Lord, to seek the Lord, indivisibly, in your whole way of life.

Exclusively

Finally, to follow God fully means to follow him exclusively. That means following others only in so far as they follow the Lord Jesus Christ, as Paul advised. As soon as a man turns away from Christ, we must turn away from that man. It means that we call no man master. It means that we strive to imitate the great saints of the Bible, people like Caleb, but only in so far as they follow the Lord Jesus Christ. We are servants only of the Lord Jesus.

Our text begins, 'But my servant Caleb'. Servants have no time of their own. They have no possessions of their own. Their silences, their speaking, their everything, belong to their master.

Caleb was a servant of God; and if you are a Christian, you are a servant of God, and everything you are, everything you own, belongs to him. You want to follow God exclusively.

Guidelines for young people

Now I am sure there are many young people who are thinking, 'This is all well and good, but do you realise how hard it is to resist all the peer pressure? When all my friends want to go to a place of sin, do you know how hard it is for me to say no?' Well, I do know how hard that is, and I do know what it is like to fall. And I do know what it is like, thank God, to go to God for repentance. You must do that, and then vow afresh, leaning on God, never to do it again.

May I give young people eight quick guidelines for fighting peer pressure, for following God fully? Here they are:

1. *Understand the strength of peer pressure*

Ralph Erskine said, 'When it comes to sin, you must do one of two things—fight or take flight.' And if you are weak in that area, you must choose flight. You must flee friends and groups and places that you know will bring you temptation, and where you find it hard to fight back. If you are strong in the area, you can go ahead and fight hand-to-hand.

2. *Lean hard on the Lord Jesus Christ*

He fought against more peer pressure than you will ever have to withstand, and he is able to give you the strength to fight in his strength.

3. *Be true to God*

Be true to God's commandments. Pray for his Holy Spirit. Think more of what God thinks of you than of what people think. Remember how small people are compared with God, and remember how small your friends are compared with God. At school you are surrounded by all those friends and you think it is so important to be accepted by them. I will tell you something: two weeks after you have graduated, you will probably never see most of those friends again. They are here today and gone tomorrow. But God never goes away. He is the inescapable God. You need to serve *him*, not people.

4. *Be true to yourself*

Give *of* yourself in friendship; that is sacrificial love. But do not give *up* yourself for friendship; that is sacrificing your convictions. Rather, use means to strengthen your convictions and strengthen your position.

5. *Remember that a true friend seeks your best*

A friend who leads you into pathways of sin is not a worthwhile friend; in fact, that person is your enemy, not your friend. You do not need those kinds of friends.

6. *Remember that long-term happiness means more than short-term pleasure*

How many older people in my congregation say things to me like this: 'If only I hadn't fallen into that sin when I was a teenager!' You know, I have worked with hundreds of seniors in my three ministries and I have never had a single senior say to me, 'I'm sorry I spent so much time when I was young serving the Lord and reading his Word and talking to his people and obeying him'—never one! But I have had a good number say to me, 'If only I'd sought the Lord when I was young. If only I hadn't caved in to peer pressure. If only I'd seen what life was all about. If only I'd lived to the glory of God. All these years the scars of my teenage sins are with me. Pardon the sins of my youth, O Lord.' Oh, young people, save yourselves from that agony and dare to say no to sin.

7. *Lead rather than be led*

You do not think your friends will respect you if you lead them in a different direction. But the truth is that they will respect you all the more, or else they will reject you altogether. And if they reject you, then that is for your best welfare at that point. Lead them in the ways of God. Be positive peer pressure for them, rather than letting them be negative peer pressure for you.

And do remember that the inner thoughts of your friends often differ from their outward words. How many times, if you are a God-fearing young person who has stood up for the Lord, have the very people who have mocked you, later come to you and said, 'You know, I'm in trouble, I wonder if you can help me'? And that is because they respect you.

8. *Remember that life is short*

Life flies by. Talk to your grandpa, talk to your grandma, ask them how quickly their lives fly by. What a tragedy to spend this one life being influenced by miserable, sinful, negative, peer pressure!

How and why Caleb followed fully

How, then, and why did Caleb follow God fully? Does it sound too good to be true—to walk all those years in such a setting in such a way? Well, our text tells us how it was possible: 'But my servant Caleb, because he had another spirit with him, and hath followed me fully, him will I bring into the land whereinto he went; and his seed shall possess it' (Numbers 14:24).

Do you hear that? 'Another spirit.' Some commentators explain it like this: the ten false spies had a spirit of distrust, of unbelief, of fear, whereas Caleb's spirit was a spirit of faith and hope. Theirs was worldly; his was heavenly. Theirs was a spirit of angry disobedience; his was a spirit of childlike obedience. Theirs was satanic; his was of God.

All this is true, but where did all these things come from? The answer can be only, of course, that Caleb had the Holy Spirit within him, and this was manifested in the whole different demeanour and spirit with which he walked before God. Paul says, 'Now we have received, not the spirit of the world, but the spirit which is of God; that we might know the things that are freely given to us of God' (1 Corinthians 2:12).

Why was the Holy Spirit given to Caleb and not to the ten false spies? Sovereign grace! And what motivates sovereign grace? Sovereign love. And what motivates sovereign love? Sovereign grace. You see, you cannot get beyond the sovereignty of God's grace and love as the source of Caleb's walk with God. God gave to Caleb the strength that he needed, and God is willing to give that strength to sinners who ask it of him.

God is a gracious God. His free gift of salvation entails within it the free gift of persevering grace, and that is through the Lord Jesus Christ. How could Caleb walk this way? Because Jesus Christ persevered to the end; because Jesus Christ followed his Father fully, in sunshine and in darkness; because Jesus Christ was exclusive in his devotion, indivisible in his walk, and persistent in his daily life. Because of Jesus Christ, Caleb received strength to be like that as well.

Friends, in ourselves we do not have the strength to be Calebs, but God has it, and God can give it to us. The Father is willing, the Son is willing, and the Spirit is willing. Will you ask it of him?

The rewards of following fully

But then, finally, our text closes with some rich promises: 'Him will I bring into the land whereinto he went; and his seed shall possess it' (Numbers 14:24). Connected with this persevering faith there are three wonderful promises.

Life

The first is that Caleb's life will be preserved. That is amazing. Over the forty years, 600,000 men and probably two and a half million people around Caleb died. Now I did not do the calculation again, but on one occasion a long time ago, when preaching on Psalm 90, I figured out that in the forty years in the wilderness there must have been something like forty funerals a day. Can you imagine seeing forty funerals a day, and people still going on murmuring for forty more years? Can you imagine living in that atmosphere? Caleb and Joshua were the only ones to survive and tell what the Lord had done. What a promise and what a reward of grace!

Now, friend, I know that as a Christian there are days when you say you will not survive. There are days when you say, with David, 'There is but a step between me and death' (1 Samuel 20:3). David was hunted for sixteen years, and maybe you feel as though you have been hunted all your life by Satan and by evil powers. But you will not be slain. God will keep you. He keeps the feet of his saints. You will survive.

God emphasises the word 'him'—the one who is following me fully—'will I [graciously] bring . . .' And the others will die. God honours them that honour him.

Land

Secondly, God promised to give Caleb the land: 'Him will I bring *into the land* whereinto he went . . .' What an amazing promise! Look at Caleb's words in Joshua 14:

And now, behold, the LORD hath kept me alive, as he said, these forty and five years, even since the LORD spake this word unto Moses, while the children of Israel wandered in the wilderness: and now, lo, I am this day fourscore and five years old. As yet I am as strong this day as I was in the day that

Moses sent me: as my strength was then, even so is my strength now, for war, both to go out, and to come in . . . Hebron therefore became the inheritance of Caleb the son of Jephunneh the Kenezite unto this day, because that he wholly followed the LORD God of Israel (verses 10-11, 14).

God gave Caleb extra strength. He rewarded his faith. Now turn to Joshua 15:14. Here is the most amazing thing of all: 'And Caleb drove thence the three sons of Anak, Sheshai, and Ahiman, and Talmai, the children of Anak.'

Who were the children of Anak? The *giants*! Who drove them out—two and a half million Israelites? 'Oh, no! We can't go in,' they said; 'two and a half million of us are not enough.' One eighty-five-year-old man is enough, if God is on his side! God plus one equals majority. 'If God be for us, who can be against us?' (Romans 8:31).

Salvation for our children

Thirdly, the Lord promises to give Caleb's seed the land to possess. The implication is obvious, is it not? Caleb's children are going to fear the Lord, and they are going to inherit the earthly Canaan as a type of the heavenly Canaan. His children will be influenced by his faith, and God will use this man for his own children. Oh, what a blessing!

One of the most gracious rewards of living a consistent life of faith, is that God uses our testimony as parents in the lives of our own children. He is a faithful, covenant-keeping God.

Dear friends, I commend you to God and to his grace. And I want to ask you in closing: Do you belong to the believing minority, or to the unbelieving majority? Do you believe that the God of Caleb still *is*?